LAND LAW

John Duddington, Worcester College of Technology

PEARSON
Longman

Harlow, England • London • New York • Boston • San Francisco • Toronto • Sydney • Singapore • Hong Kong
Tokyo • Seoul • Taipei • New Delhi • Cape Town • Madrid • Mexico City • Amsterdam • Munich • Paris • Milan

Pearson Education Limited
Edinburgh Gate
Harlow
Essex CM20 2JE
England

and Associated Companies throughout the world

Visit us on the World Wide Web at:
www.pearsoned.co.uk
First published 2007

ISBN–13: 978-1 40584-021-7
ISBN–10: 1-40584-021-8

British Library Cataloguing-in-Publication Data
A catalogue record for this book is available from the British Library

Library of Congress Cataloging-in-Publication Data
A catalogue record for this book is avaiable from the Library of Congress

10 9 8 7 6 5 4 3 2 1
10 09 08 07

Typeset in Helvetica Condensed by 3
Printed by Ashford Colour Press Ltd., Gosport

The publisher's policy is to use paper manufactured from sustainable forests.

Visit the *Law Express Series* Companion Website at **www.pearsoned.co.uk/lawexpress** to find valuable **student** learning material including:

- A Study Plan test to assess how well you know the subject before you begin your revision
- Interactive quizzes to test your knowledge of the main points from each chapter of the book
- Diagram plans for the questions in each chapter of the book
- Further examination questions and guidelines for answering them
- Interactive flashcards to help you revise the main cases
- Printable versions of the topic maps and checklists

Contents

Supporting resources
Visit **www.pearsoned.co.uk/lawexpress** to find valuable online resources

Companion Website for students
- A Study Plan test to assess how well you know the subject before you begin your revision
- Interactive quizzes to test your knowledge of the main points from each chapter of the book
- Diagram plans for the questions in each chapter of the book
- Further examination questions and guidelines for answering them
- Interactive flashcards to help you revise the main cases
- Printable versions of the topic maps and checklists

Also: The Companion Website provides the following features:

- Search tool to help locate specific items of content
- E-mail results and profile tools to send results of quizzes to instructors
- Online help and support to assist with website usage and troubleshooting

For more information please contact your local Pearson Education sales representative or visit **www.pearsoned.co.uk/lawexpress**

Introduction

■ Some general issues

Let us go straight to the point. Students are either Land Law enthusiasts or they think of it with fear. This book is intended for both types of students as a guide to how to gain the best possible mark in their exams.

Land Law enthusiasts will agree with me that this is one of the most fascinating of all legal subjects. It is rich in variety, full of interesting issues and, more than in some areas of law, it is of direct relevance to us all.

Those students who fear the subject should remember the following points (enthusiasts will find them useful too):

■ There are fewer cases in Land Law than in most other legal subjects. You do not need to learn vast numbers of obscure cases – just know the main ones well and be able to apply them to questions.

■ Land Law is much more statute based than, for example, Contract, Tort or Equity.

■ The fact that this is so means that there is more certainty, although it also means that you must be able to recall vital statutory provisions accurately.

■ Problem questions usually (but not always) have a right or wrong answer. This can be a help, especially if you are not so confident about this subject.

Despite this, there remain two reasons why students do find this subject difficult, and this guide tries to overcome both of them:

1 The language is off-putting. Immediately you begin to study this subject you are confronted with terms like 'estates' and 'interests', and interests which mysteriously subdivide into 'legal' and 'equitable'. Then land registration rules have terms of their own, such as land charges, overriding and minor interests.

2 The structure is difficult to understand: how do the basic ideas of estates and interests fit into the land registration rules and how do the rules themselves work?

These are particular problems which are dealt with in the material covered in the first three chapters: estates and interests in land, registered land and unregistered land. If you can master these then you will have gone a long way to achieving a reasonable pass in your exam as most questions will involve some knowledge of these areas. Make revision based on these chapters one of your last jobs before the Land Law exam.

What does this guide do to help?

▌ It takes you through the fundamental areas step by step and encourages you not to go on to the next area until you have mastered the one before.

▌ It links different areas by using the same problem question for the first three chapters, showing you how the law builds up, and by revision notes which clearly point you to other linked areas of the syllabus.

▌ It highlights key cases, statutes and definitions.

▌ Each chapter has a visual map which clearly shows you how each topic develops.

What this guide cannot do is to:

▌ Do away with the need to learn the material thoroughly and be able to use it in the exam. Only you can do this, but this guide aims to make your task as painless as possible.

▌ Act as a substitute for the standard textbooks.

▌General essay question advice

The same advice applies to answering Land Law essay questions as it does to all other essay questions: answer the actual question and address the issues which it raises. For example, suppose that you were faced with this question:

'The object of the system of land registration is to ensure that a purchaser will be safe in relying on the register.'

Discuss whether the present system of land registration achieves this aim.

Do not, on any account, begin by simply describing the system, e.g. by ploughing through minor interests, overriding interests, etc. Here you are just describing the system. Essay questions at this level ask for more than this.

Do, first, note that the question refers to the present system i.e. under the Land Registration Act 2002 – you will get credit for pointing this out – and, second, deal with the issue posed in the quotation. You will get more guidance on this both in this book and on the accompanying website. A useful tip is that Land Law exams nearly always have an essay question on land registration, so have some points ready!

▌General problem question advice

In answering any problem question, follow these steps. If you do, you are bound to address the main preliminary issues and so get your answer off to a good start:

▌ Identify the right involved – Chapter 1 gives a list of proprietary and personal rights. Memorise them.

▌ Check if any interest in the land is legal or equitable.

▌ Check if title to the land is registered or unregistered.

This drill applies throughout the subject, e.g. to questions on leases, licences, easements, profits and mortgages. It will not take you all the way, but it will give you a good basis.

Remember that, as was said above, problem questions in Land Law exams usually have a right or wrong answer, so ensure that your answer has a good, logical structure leading to a clear conclusion.

The 'Land Law Box'

When answering problem questions, *always* think of *all* the issues in the box:

```
                    LEGAL ESTATES



    LEGAL INTERESTS           EQUITABLE INTERESTS



    REGISTERED TITLE          UNREGISTERED TITLE
```

This time: think INSIDE the box!

Two vital statutes:

Make yourself familiar with these!

Law of Property Act 1925 – still the foundation of land law terminology – abbreviated to LPA in this book.

Land Registration Act 2002 – foundation of the system of land registration – abbreviated to LRA 2002 in this book.

Guided Tour

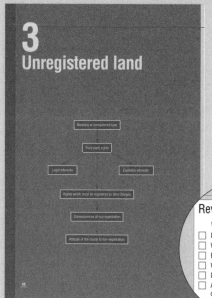

Topic maps – Highlight the main points and allow you to find your way quickly and easily through each chapter.

Revision checklist – How well do you know each topic? Don't panic if you don't know them all, the chapters will help you to revise each point so that you will be fully prepared for your exams.

Revision checklist

What you need to know:

- [ ] Difference between unregistered and re
- [ ] Which rights must be registered as land
- [ ] Effect of non-registration
- [ ] Which rights are not registrable as lan
- [ ] Division of these rights into legal and
- [ ] Are purchasers bound by legal inter charges?
- [ ] Are purchasers bound by eq

Sample questions – Prepare for what you will be faced with in your exams! Guidance on structuring strong answers is provided at the end of the chapter.

Problem question advice
Problem questions may link with other areas or be self-contained. An obvious area to link to is trusts of the home (Chapter 5), where you could be required to decide if a party has an equitable interest and then to decide if it is overriding. Even a self-contained question (such as the one below) will involve knowledge of the material in Chapter 1.

Key definition boxes – Make sure you understand essential legal terms.

KEY DEFINITION
A **restrictive covenant** exists where a person covenants in a deed not to use his land in a certain way or to do something on his land, e.g. to keep fences in repair or not to build on the land. See Chapter 10.

Problem area boxes – Highlight areas where students most often trip up in exams. Use them to make sure you do not make the same mistakes.

A contractual licence is where a l...

Problem area

At common law, contractual licences and ba... at any time, although equitable remedies ma... no problem with bare licences but where a p... seemed unfair for it be capable of being rev... case law.

Example

...pay £100 for a ticket to a Test Mat... ...ound and am just starting... ...the reason h...

Mortgage Corporation Ltd v. *Shaire* [2001] 4 All ER 364

Concerning: application of the principles in s.15 TLATA 1996

Facts

The house was held by X and Y as joint tenants. It was bought to provide a home for them and Y's son by a previous marriage. X owned a 25% share in equity and Y a 75% share. X mortgaged the house by forging Y's signature and after X's death the mortgagee sought a sale. The court refused.

Legal principle

By comparison with the previous law, Parliament had intended to 'tip the scales more in favour of families and against banks and other chargees' (Neuberger J). Nevertheless, the cases under the old law (s.30 LPA 1925) can still be referred to, albeit with caution.

The case does not establish an absolute principle that family rights come first: see e.g. *Pritchard Engelfield* v. *Steinberg* (2004), where the mortgagee did obtain a sale.

Key case and key statutory provision boxes – Identify the essential cases and statutes that you need to know for your exams.

Section 15 of the TLATA 1996

Sets out the following criteria to which the courts must have regard when settling disputes (in practice, and certainly in examination questions, these are particularly relevant when looking at disputes over whether land should be sold):

'(a) the intentions of the person or persons (if any) who created the trust,
(b) the purposes for which the property subject to the trust is held,
(c) the welfare of any minor who occupies, or might reasonably be expected to occupy any land subject to the trust as his home, and
(d) the interests of any secured creditor of any beneficiary.'

Further thinking boxes – Illustrate areas of academic debate, and point you towards that extra reading required for the top grades.

FURTHER THINKING

In *State Bank of India* v. *Sood* (1997) it was held that overreaching applies not only where capital money is actually paid but also where a mortgage of land is created as security for an existing debt. See (1997) CLJ 494 for discussion of this point.

Glossary – Forgotten the meaning of a word? – Where a word is highlighted in the text, turn to the glossary at the back of the book to remind yourself of its meaning.

Glossary of terms

Key definitions

Absolute	Appears to have no meaning beyond the fact that a term of years may be absolute even if it contains a clause enabling either party to determine it by notice.
Bare licence	Licence given without any consideration from the licensee i.e. when you are invited to someone's house for a party.
Contractual licence	Where a licence is given for consideration.
Covenants	Promises in a deed.
Easement	Gives a person the right to use the land of another in some way or to prevent it being used for certain purposes e.g. rights of way and rights of water and light.

Exam tips – Want to impress examiners? These indicate how you can improve your exam performance and your chances of getting top marks.

EXAM TIP

If you get a problem question on the lines of the facts in *Kingsnorth Trust Ltd* v. *Tizard* (i.e. rights of beneficiaries under a trust of land), check first how many persons are transferring the legal estate. If it is one, there cannot be overreaching. More than one, and overreaching will take place.

Revision notes – Highlight points that you should be aware of in other topic areas, or where your own course may adopt a specific approach that you should check with your course tutor before reading further.

REVISION NOTE

Check Chapter 1 and especially *Kingsnorth Finance* v. *Tizard* and compare the solution there with that in Sch.3, para. 2 above.

In a typical question based on *Williams & Glyn's Bank Ltd* v. *Boland* (1980) (see below) you should approach a problem question in this way:

Table of cases and statutes

Cases

Statutes

Dedication and acknowledgements

To my father, Walter Duddington, who first encouraged me to become a lawyer, and who would, I think, have enjoyed Land Law; to my wife, Anne, for the constant support, loyalty and technical expertise without which my books would never begin to be written; to my daughter, Mary, for her seemingly faultless proofreading and sense of fun which keeps me going; and to my son, Christopher, for just being himself.

I would also like to thank the staff of Pearson, especially Rebekah Taylor and Cheryl Cheasley, for their endless encouragement, cheerfulness and practical guidance, and all reviewers who contributed to the development of this text, including students participating in research and focus groups which helped to shape the series format.

John Duddington
July 2006

Publisher's acknowledgment

We would like to thank all reviewers who contributed to the development of this text, including students participating in research and focus groups who helped shape the series format.

1

The building blocks of land law: estates and interests in land

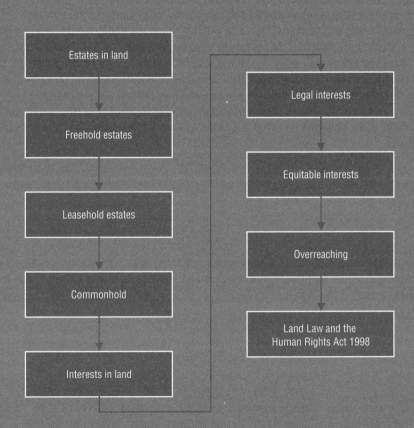

Estates in land

Freehold estates

Leasehold estates

Commonhold

Interests in land

Legal interests

Equitable interests

Overreaching

Land Law and the Human Rights Act 1998

Revision checklist

What you need to know:

- [ ] What the term 'estate' means
- [ ] What the term 'freehold' means
- [ ] What the term 'leasehold' means
- [ ] The two types of legal estates
- [ ] Distinction between estates and interests in land
- [ ] Types of legal interests in land
- [ ] Types of equitable interests in land
- [ ] When a legal interest binds a third party
- [ ] When an equitable interest binds a third party
- [ ] When overreaching can apply and its consequences

Introduction
Understanding the foundations of land law

A clear understanding of this topic is absolutely essential for a pass in a land law exam. It deals with the fundamental building blocks of land law: the estates and interests which can exist in land. You must know what these terms mean and which rights can be estates and which can be interests.

This chapter and the next two (on registration of title to land and interests in land) should be thought of as one: this chapter is the essential foundation and then leads on to either registered or unregistered land.

Essay question advice

An essay question will probably ask you either to:

- Look at the distinction between legal estates and legal and equitable interests and explain the significance of each. *OR*
- Look at the background to the development of land law as it is today. Here you will need to have read widely on the law before the 1925 property law reforms and be able to evaluate how successful they have been and the need for future changes. This answer may require knowledge of other areas dealt with in subsequent chapters, such as land registration rules (Chapters 2 and 3).

You will be unlikely to get a problem question purely on the material in this chapter, as it is introductory. However, in a problem question on either unregistered or registered land you will require a sound knowledge of the material here.

Students often find a problem in relating the material in this chapter to the rules on registered and unregistered land. Simply regard this material as the foundations of land law: you cannot build the house with it but the house will not stand up unless you know it. Concentrate on making absolutely sure that you are clear about all the material in this chapter before you go on to the next one: do not worry about registration of land rules until you come to them!

To help you in seeing how the rules in Chapters 1, 2 and 3 relate to each other, there is the same problem question for each chapter: in this chapter we will see how the various interests in land work in themselves and then in the next two chapters we will look at the impact of them on the land registration rules.

Sample questions

Could you answer these questions? Have a look at the questions which follow. They are examples of a typical essay question and a typical problem question. This chapter will cover the issues raised in these questions and review the law necessary to provide a comprehensive answer. Guidelines on answering the problem question will be provided at the end of the chapter and guidelines on answering the essay question are on the companion website for this book.

Essay question

Distinguish between legal and equitable interests in land. What is the importance of the distinction?

Problem question

John has bought a freehold house with some farmland from Steve.

After John's purchase, Fred, Susie and Jean, who are all neighbours, come to see him with letters signed by Steve.

Fred has a letter granting him the right to cut wood from trees on the land.

Susie has a letter agreeing to grant her a two-year lease of one acre of the farmland, rent payable yearly. Susie has not started to use the land.

Jean has a letter stating that she has a licence to park her caravan on the land.

In addition, Elsie, Steve's mother arrives and says that she paid half the purchase price when Steve bought the house and so she has a right to stay there. Elsie was away on holiday when John purchased the house.

Advise John on whether he is bound by any of these claims.

■Estates in land

The fundamental principle of Land Law is that all land is owned by the Crown. The most that anyone can have is an *estate* in the land.

KEY DEFINITIONS

An **estate in land** refers to the rights which a person has to control and use the land. An **estate owner** is often called the owner of the land.

There are two estates:

■ Freehold.
■ Leasehold.

Difference between freehold and leasehold:

■ Freehold estates last for an unlimited time and in practice they are perpetual.
■ Leasehold estates last for a definite time.

Note one common characteristic of estates in land: They must be created by deed (see below) except in the case of leases for up to three years (s.54(2) LPA 1925).

REVISION NOTE

Check Chapter 7 and revise the methods of creation of a lease.

KEY STATUTORY PROVISION

Section 1(1) of the LPA 1925

'The only estates in land which are capable of subsisting or of being created or conveyed at law are –
(a) An estate in fee simple absolute in possession [legal freehold estate];
(b) A term of years absolute [legal leasehold estate].'

Freehold estates

A freehold estate is the nearest to absolute ownership recognised by English law.

KEY DEFINITIONS

The **fee simple absolute in possession**.
These terms mean:
fee – can be inherited
simple – by anyone
absolute – will not end on a certain event, i.e. to X until he marries
in possession – not, e.g. to X at 21 and X is now 19

Before 1925 there were a number of legal estates of freehold but not all of them could be freely bought and sold, e.g. land might be held by Y for life only and would have to be passed on his son. There were ways of freeing land from these restrictions but it was thought better that all land held in freehold should be capable of being freely transferred; i.e. if the freehold owner wishes to transfer the land, then there should be no legal reason why he should not be able to do so. This is a fundamental principle of land law.

It is still possible to have other freehold estates but they can only exist behind a trust (see below).

All land must have a freehold owner and if the individual owner cannot be traced, the ownership is held by the Crown.

Leasehold estates

Land may also be held under a leasehold estate and so there will be two estates in the same land: the freehold and the leasehold.
The term of years absolute:

KEY DEFINITIONS

Term of years means any period having a fixed and certain duration. **Absolute** appears to have no meaning beyond the fact that a term of years may be absolute even if it contains a clause enabling either party to determine it by notice.

FURTHER THINKING

You may get an essay question on the historical development of land law and if so you should concentrate on:

▌ Why was the LPA 1925 passed?
▌ Does it need further reform?

This may be linked with the system of land registration – in particular the LRA 2002 has updated this – see Chapter 2.
For a really good mark, look at Simpson, *A History of the Land Law*, Oxford University Press, 2nd edition, 1986.

Commonhold

The concept of commonhold was introduced by the Commonhold and Leasehold Reform Act 2002, Part 1 of which, dealing with commonhold, came into force on 27 September 2004. You are less likely to get a whole question on this but an answer to an essay question on the general principles of land law will gain extra marks if you mention commonhold. You should remember that:

▌ Until now, flats have been held under leases rather than freeholds because it is difficult to enforce positive covenants between freehold owners (see Chapter 10) but they can be enforced if they are in leases.
▌ The introduction of commonhold is intended to allow freehold ownership of flats.
▌ Commonhold is not a new legal estate in land (i.e. there are still just two) but it is a new method of owning freehold land.
▌ The commonhold system allows properties such as blocks of flats to be registered at the Land Registry as commonhold land.
▌ The owner of each unit (i.e. each flat) will be registered as the freehold owner.
▌ Each owner will be a member of a commonhold association.
▌ The association will be a company and will be the freehold owner of the common parts e.g. the stairs.
▌ Therefore, the ownership is split between the individual flat owners and the commonhold association which owns the common parts.

FURTHER READING

See Smith (2004) Conv 194 for a discussion and analysis of commonhold.

▌Interests in land

KEY DEFINITION

An **interest in land** is a right which a person has over another's land.

Remember that by contrast an estate in land is a right which a person has over their land. There are two types of interests in land:

▌ Legal interests.
▌ Equitable interests.

Those interests which are legal are set out below, and all other interests must be equitable. As mentioned above, it is vital when studying land law not to go on to a new point before you are absolutely clear about the present one. Do not think about equitable interests until you have mastered what is meant by legal interests.

Legal and equitable interests in land have one common feature: They are *proprietary* rights in land. This means that they attach to property (i.e. land) and so are capable of binding third parties who acquire the land.

Personal rights in land are different: they can, in general, only be binding on the persons who agreed to them. An example of a personal right often met in land law is a licence to use land. This amounts to permission to use the land but will not be binding on a purchaser of the land.

REVISION NOTE

Licences are dealt with in Chapter 8, where you will see that there is some argument about whether certain licences are proprietary, but the examples given in earlier chapters of this book will involve licences which are undoubtedly only personal.

Example

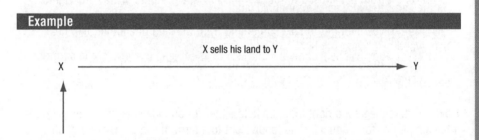

Z has an easement over X's land. This is an example of a proprietary right and so is capable of binding Y when X sells his land to him.

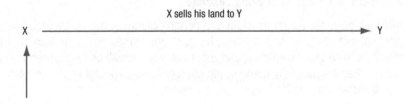

Z has permission from X to sit in X's garden and paint the view of the hills. This is only a licence and so it is a personal right and cannot be binding on Y.

Legal interests in land

Note: These are defined in s.1(2) of the LPA 1925. Only these can be legal. All interests not in this list must be equitable.

EXAM TIP

For an essay question you should know all the legal interests, but only the interests in (a) and (c) below (easements, profits and mortgages) are likely to appear in problem questions.

The list of interests which *can be* legal is:

(a) **an easement, right or privilege in or over land for an interest equivalent to an estate in fee simple absolute in possession or a term of years absolute.**

This includes both easements and profits a prendre.

KEY DEFINITIONS

An **easement** gives a person the right to use the land of another in some way or to prevent it from being used for certain purposes, e.g. rights of way and rights of water and light.

A **profit** gives the right to take something from the land of another, e.g. peat, fish, wood or grazing rights.

You need to be absolutely clear about the distinction between these. Easements and profits are dealt with in Chapter 9.

However, to be legal the right must be held either for an indefinite time (equivalent to a fee simple) or for a definite time (equivalent to a term of years). Therefore, an easement for life or a right of drainage granted until the road is adopted by the local authority cannot be a legal interest and must be equitable.

(b) **A rentcharge in possession issuing out of or charged on land being either perpetual or for a term of years absolute.**

A rentcharge gives the owner the right to a periodical sum of money secured on land independently of any lease or mortgage. No new rentcharges can be created after 22 July 1977 (with certain exceptions) and most rentcharges will be extinguished on 22 July 2037. They are generally found in the Manchester and Bristol areas. The same rules on whether they are legal apply as in easements.

(c) **Charge by way of legal mortgage.**

KEY DEFINITION

A **mortgage** is a charge on land to secure a debt.

This is one of the ways of creating a legal mortgage (see Chapter 11).

(d) **Land tax, tithe rentcharge, and *any other* similar *charge on land which is not created by an instrument.***

The common feature of any charges coming within this provision is that they are periodical payments with which land was burdened by law. The three specific charges which fell within this provision have been abolished. The part italicised above is all that remains.

(e) **Rights of entry exercisable over or in respect of a legal term of years absolute, or annexed, for any purpose, to a legal rentcharge.**

A right of re-entry in a lease if the tenant, for example, fails to pay the rent, is made an interest in land in itself. It is often attached to a legal rentcharge to secure payment of the rent.

Assuming that the interest is within this list, then in order to be legal it must be created by deed.

KEY STATUTORY PROVISION

Section 52 (1) of the LPA 1925

'All conveyances of land or of any interest therein are void for the purposes of conveying or creating a legal estate unless made by deed.'

A deed is a document which, if made before 31 July 1990, had to be sealed, but this is no longer necessary.

KEY STATUTORY PROVISION

Section 1(2) and (3) of the Law of Property (Miscellaneous Provisions) Act 1989

'(2) An instrument shall not be a deed unless –
(a) it makes clear ... that it is intended to be a deed ...
(3) (a) it is signed [by the person executing it] in the presence of a witness who attests the signature ...
(b) it is delivered [by the person executing it or by someone on his behalf] as a deed.'

Example One

X agrees with Y by a deed that Y can have a right of way across X's land for the rest of Y's life.
Step One: Identify the right – an easement.
Step Two: Is it legal or equitable? – as it is for life it can only be equitable, even if it is in a deed.

Example Two

X by deed grants a right of way across X's land.
Step One: Identify the right – an easement.
Step Two: Is it legal or equitable? As it does not say that the easement is only for Y's life, we can assume that it is for ever. So it can be legal or equitable.
Step Three: Is it in a deed? Yes, so it is legal.

Equitable interests in land

All other interests in land are equitable.

KEY DEFINITION

The term **equitable** means that the right was originally only recognised by the Court of Chancery, which dealt with equitable rights, and not by the Courts of Common Law.

You do not need to know equity in detail in order to pass exams in Land Law, but you should keep this fundamental characteristic of equity in mind:

Equity often applied where the application of the strict rules of the common law would not have produced a just result. The effect was that equity often did not insist on the observance of formalities such as the need for a right to be granted in a deed (above). You can find out more about equity in the companion book to this one: *Law Express: Equity and Trusts*.

In Land Law exams you should ask two questions to decide if the right is equitable:

■ Is it in the above list of legal interests? If not, then it must be equitable.
■ If it is in the above list, then was it created by deed? If not, then it must be equitable.

REVISION NOTE

Chapter 3 also deals with another way in which a right can become equitable rather than legal: if it is not registered as required by the LRA 2002. Keep this point at the back of your mind for now, but do not worry about registered land yet.

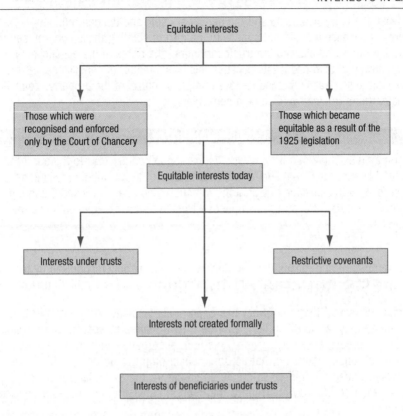

Interest under trusts

A **trust** arises when property is held by one person (the trustee) on trust for another (the beneficiary).

X (trustee) ──────────────────────────► Y (beneficiary)

X is the legal owner but Y has the equitable interest.

In a trust, the legal ownership and the benefit are split and the common law, apparently because it could not cope with the idea of splitting these two, refused to recognise trusts and allowed the trustee to ignore the rights of the beneficiaries. Equity, however, enforced trusts because this was a matter of conscience, i.e. the trustee had never been intended to have complete control of the property. You will find later that a trustee can also be a beneficiary.

REVISION NOTE

A common example of a trust is where a person (Y) contributes to the purchase price of land but the legal title is held in the name of X. X will hold the land on trust for Y in the absence of a contrary intention. See Chapters 3 and 5 and the *Tizard* case below. Keep this example of a trust in mind: it is frequently met in Land Law.

Interests not created formally

Principle: Provided that a contract has been made to create an interest in land, then equity may, at its discretion, enforce it by a decree of *specific performance* or restrain its breach by an *injunction*. This is in accordance with the equitable maxim that 'equity looks on that as done which ought to be done'. This means that when a deed is required to create an estate or interest in land then if there is no deed then equity may still regard the interest subsisting in land as an equitable interest.

Example

X agrees to grant Y a right of way over his land. This is not in a deed. As in the example on page 10 we can assume that it is to last for ever, as it does not say that it is for life. However, the lack of a deed would still be fatal to it being a legal easement. However, equity may come to the rescue and declare it to be an equitable easement. Another example is an agreement for a lease.

EXAM TIP

How to tell if there is a deed or just an agreement:
    The word 'grants' usually indicates a deed, as this is the idea behind one: the right of way is granted by X to Y and not agreed by them.
    The words 'agrees to grant' indicates just an agreement, as it points to the future and this fits with the idea behind equity: it enforces a contract to grant an interest in the future.

Section 2 of the Law of Property (Miscellaneous Provisions) Act 1989

This provides that contracts for the sale or other disposition of an interest in land made on or after 27 September 1989 must satisfy the following requirements:

■ be in writing,
■ contain all the terms agreed by the parties; and
■ be signed by all the parties.

Therefore, equity will enforce a contract for, for example, an equitable easement provided that it satisfies these requirements. Contracts made before that date do not require writing and there are a number of fairly recent cases when this point has been important. Another example of an equitable interest in this connection is an *estate contract* which is a contract to convey a legal estate.

Note: Effect of electronic conveyancing on the formalities required for deeds and contracts set out above.

Section 91 of the LRA 2002 provides that, in order to pave the way for the introduction of electronic conveyancing (see Chapter 2), electronic documents will be capable of satisfying these requirements. The details have not all been worked out, but it is likely that each person will have an electronic signature.

Restrictive covenants

KEY DEFINITION

A restrictive covenant exists where a person covenants in a deed not to use his land in a certain way or to do something on his land, e.g. to keep fences in repair or not to build on the land. See Chapter 10.

These have only ever been enforced in equity.

REVISION NOTE

Rights created by equitable estoppel may also be regarded as equitable interests – see Chapter 8.

Why do you need to know the distinction between legal and equitable interests?

This is because of the different effects which they have on a purchaser of the land and on third parties.

KEY DEFINITION

Legal interests are binding on all the world, i.e. on everyone who buys the land.

KEY DEFINITION

Equitable interests are not binding on a bona fide purchaser for value without notice.

What does *bona fide purchaser for value without notice* mean?

Bona fide means that the purchaser must be in good faith. It may mean that a person who buys for an improper purpose would not be protected but see *Midland Bank* v. *Green* (*No 3*) (1981) (in Chapter 3).

Purchaser for value means that some value must be given and this includes money, money's worth and marriage. A donee (who takes by gift) would not take free of an equitable interest.

Notice. This is the most important requirement. Notice means any of the following:

(a) Actual notice, i.e. actual knowledge.
(b) Constructive notice. This has two elements:
  (i) A purchaser is bound by any matters which would be revealed by an examination of the deeds. As a result of this rule it is common for a note of equitable interests to be made on the back of deeds.
  (ii) A purchaser is bound by all matters which would be revealed by an inspection of the land. (Rule in *Hunt* v. *Luck* (1901)).
(c) Imputed notice. This means that a purchaser has notice of any matters of which his agent has notice as in *Tizard* (below) where the mortgagee was bound by the knowledge of the surveyor.

Kingsnorth Trust Ltd v. *Tizard* [1986] 2 All ER 54

Concerning: constructive notice of equitable interests in unregistered land

Facts

An agent of the mortgagee who carried out an inspection of the matrimonial home, which was in the name of the mortgagor, was bound by the equitable interest of the mortgagor's wife, as he had constructive notice of it. Two points ought to have led the agent to make further enquiries:

■ He had found evidence that the couple's children were in occupation.
■ The mortgagor described himself as single in the mortgage application form but then told the agent that he was separated from his wife, who was living nearby.

A further point which should have led the agent to enquire further was that he inspected the house at a time (Sunday) arranged in advance with the mortgagor.

Legal principle

A purchaser will have constructive notice of any rights which are discoverable by making reasonable enquiries.

REVISION NOTE

Do remember that this case concerned unregistered land, which is covered in Chapter 3. If title to the land had been registered, the wife would have claimed that she had an overriding interest in the land under what is now Sch.3(2) to the LRA 2002 (interests of persons in actual occupation).

REVISION NOTE

The wife's claim to an equitable interest in the house was based on her contribution to the purchase price of a house which had been previously owned by the couple, the proceeds of which had been used to buy the present house. These facts are therefore a good example of how an equitable interest in property can be acquired in this way. Look at Chapter 5 and especially *Lloyds Bank* v. *Rosset* (1990).

EXAM TIP

A frequent exam problem question asks you to decide if an equitable interest in property was acquired and then asks you to look at a situation similar to that in the above case on the basis that title to the land is either registered or unregistered. This means that you must have a good knowledge of Chapters 2, 3 and 5. Do not be tempted to leave any of these out when revising!

Note that if a person is not a purchaser then they take the land with all equitable rights.

EXAM TIP

Check in a question whether a person has, e.g., inherited the land. If so, they will not be a purchaser.

Overreaching

KEY DEFINITION

Overreaching is the process by which equitable rights which exist under a trust of land are removed from the land and transferred to the money (called capital money) which has just been paid to purchase the land. The effect is to give the purchaser automatic priority over equitable interests under a trust.

KEY STATUTORY PROVISION

Section 2(1) of the LPA 1925

'A conveyance to a purchaser of a legal estate in land shall overreach any equitable interest or power affecting that estate, whether or not he has notice thereof . . .

Note carefully this vital restriction on overreaching: it can only take place if the transaction is made by at least two trustees or a trust corporation. See also Section 27 LPA 1925.

Examples

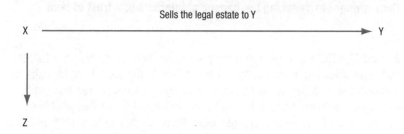

Sells the legal estate to Y

X ─────────────────────────────────────► Y

│
▼
Z

Z has an interest under a trust of land, as Mrs Tizard did in *Kingsnorth* v. *Tizard*. Y will be bound by Z's interest if he/she has notice of it (see above).

Now change the example:

X and W ─────────────────────────────────────► Y

│
▼
Z

Z has an interest under a trust of land.

Here Y will not be bound by Z's interest even if Y had notice of it as the transaction was entered into by two trustees (X and W) and so Z's interest in the property is overreached and is transferred to the proceeds of sale. The effect is that Y need not concern himself about them but Z may claim against X and W for any share of the proceeds of sale which she feels belongs to her.

EXAM TIP

If you get a problem question on the lines of the facts in *Kingsnorth Trust Ltd* v. *Tizard* (i.e. rights of beneficiaries under a trust of land), check first how many persons are transferring the legal estate. If it is one, there cannot be overreaching. More than one, and overreaching will take place.

City of London Building Society v. *Flegg* **[1987] 3 All ER 465**

Concerning: overreaching the beneficial interests in a trust of land

Facts

Mr and Mrs MB were the registered proprietors of a house but over half the purchase price had been raised by Mr and Mrs F, the parents of Mrs MB and who were also to live at the house. Accordingly, the house was held on trust for all four of them. Mr and Mrs MB then, without the knowledge of her parents, raised two further charges over the property and they then defaulted on the repayments. The lender sought possession and it was held that the interests of the parents had been overreached by the charges and their rights now only existed in the proceeds of sale.

Legal principle

The interests of beneficiaries in a trust of land are overreached if the transaction is entered into by two or more trustees.

Note that under S.205(1)(xxi) of the LPA a purchaser includes a person who acquires a charge by way of legal mortgage, i.e. in practice, a lender under a mortgage.

FURTHER THINKING

In *State Bank of India* v. *Sood* (1997) it was held that overreaching applies not only where capital money is actually paid but also where a mortgage of land is created as security for an existing debt. See (1997) CLJ 494 for discussion of this point.

■ Land Law and the Human Rights Act 1998

You can boost your marks in a Land Law exam by showing knowledge of the applicability of the Human Rights Act 1998.

The following parts of the European Convention on Human Rights are especially relevant:

Article 1 of the First Protocol: No one shall be deprived of his possessions except in the public interest and subject to the conditions provided for by law and the general principles of International law.

Article 8: Right to respect to private and family life.

REVISION NOTE

See Chapters 3 and 6 for examples of the possible application of these provisions.

FURTHER THINKING

Read Gray in Tee (ed.) *Land Law: Issues, Debates, Policy* (Willan Publishing, 2002), pp. 221–45.

▌Chapter summary
▌Putting it all together

Answer guidelines

See problem question at the start of the chapter.

Steve ———————————————————————————→ John

Fred/Susie/Jean/Elsie: Are their rights binding on John?

Decide the category into which each interest falls:

Fred: Profit: not legal – not in a deed so must be equitable.
Susie: Lease: not legal – not in a deed so must be equitable – estate contract.
Jean: Licence – not a proprietary right at all so cannot bind John.
Elsie: May have right under a trust so equitable interest.

As these are equitable interests, apply the rules on whether John has notice of them and so is bound by them.

Make your answer stand out
Ask whether they are purchasers or not – if not, John cannot be bound. This simple point is often ignored by students!

2
Registered land

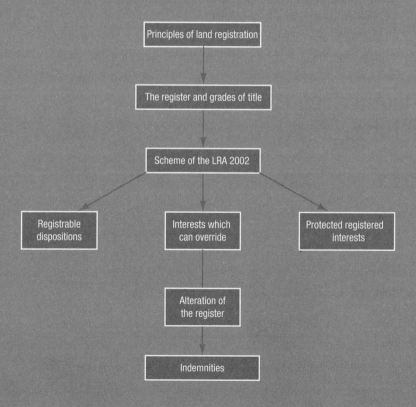

Principles of land registration

The register and grades of title

Scheme of the LRA 2002

Registrable dispositions

Interests which can override

Protected registered interests

Alteration of the register

Indemnities

Revision checklist

What you need to know:

- [ ] What is meant by registration of title to land
- [ ] How registered land differs from unregistered land
- [ ] Principles of land registration
- [ ] The grades of title
- [ ] Which dispositions must be completed by registration
- [ ] What is meant by the term 'interests which can override'
- [ ] Which interests can override on first registration
- [ ] Which interests can override on subsequent registration
- [ ] What is meant by the term 'protected registered interests'
- [ ] How such interests can be protected
- [ ] Outline when the register can be altered
- [ ] Outline when there is a claim to an indemnity under the LRA 2002

Introduction
Understanding registered land

This is the indispensable topic of Land Law. Land registration will come into virtually all problem questions:

- Adverse possession
- Leases
- Licences by estoppel
- Easements and profits
- Freehold covenants
- Mortgages

It can also form the subject of an essay question.

Essay question advice

The obvious areas for essay questions, which overlap to some extent, are:

- The LRA 2002: how has it changed the system of registered land and how far has it been successful?
- The existence of overriding interests: should they still exist?
- A comparison between the systems of registered and unregistered land.

Problem question advice

Problem questions may link with other areas or be self-contained. An obvious area to link to is trusts of the home (Chapter 5), where you could be required to decide if a party has an equitable interest and then to decide if it is overriding. Even a self-contained question (such as the one below) will involve knowledge of the material in Chapter 1.

Sample questions

Essay question

The object of the Land Registration Acts is that title to land is to be ascertainable from the register alone.

To what extent does the Land Registration Act 2002 meet this objective?

Problem question

John has bought a freehold house with some farmland from Steve.

After John's purchase, Fred, Susie and Jean, who are all neighbours, come to see him with letters signed by Steve.

(a) Fred has a letter granting him the right to cut wood from trees on the land.

(b) Susie has a letter agreeing to grant her a two-year lease of one acre of the farmland, rent payable yearly. Susie has not started to use the land.

(c) Jean has a letter stating that she has a licence to park her caravan on the land.

In addition, Elsie, Steve's mother, arrives and says that she paid half the purchase price when Steve bought the house and so she has a right to stay there. Elsie was away on holiday when John purchased the house.

Advise John on whether he is bound by any of these claims.

■ Principles of land registration

An essay question in an exam may ask you to explain the principles of land registration. You need to emphasise that the Land Registration Act 1925 (LRA) provided for a system of registration of titles and not title to land. Therefore, as we see below, there may be more than one title applicable to the same piece of land. The LRA 1925 has now been repealed and replaced by the LRA 2002, which retains and indeed strengthens the system of land registration. **The vital difference from the unregistered system, which is dealt with in the next chapter, is that here title to land is registered rather than just charges against the estate owner who holds the title deeds.** The intention is that all land shall be held under registered title as soon as practicable.

The other main aim of the Act is to make arrangements in the legislation to enable dispositions of registered land to be dealt with electronically. The details of this have yet to be worked out but it is likely that there will be a secure intranet system operating through the internet with secure software protected protocols. It is most unlikely that you will need to discuss this in detail.

The land registration scheme rests on three principles:

■ **Mirror principle** – all facts relevant to the title are to be found on the register.
■ **Curtain principle** – purchasers need not look beyond the register and are not concerned with trusts.
■ **Insurance principle** – any flaw in the register leads to the payment of compensation to a person affected.

■The register and grades of title

The register

This is divided into three parts:

(a) Property register

This:
■ contains a verbal description of the land and a description by reference to a plan
■ identifies the estate comprised in the title (freehold or leasehold)
■ notes any rights which benefit the land, e.g. easements and restrictive covenants of which the registered land is the dominant tenement.

(b) Proprietorship register

This:
■ states the nature of the title (see below)
■ states the name and address of the registered proprietor (RP)
■ sets out any restrictions which affect the power of the RP to deal with the land, e.g. he is a trustee or a bankrupt.

(c) Charges register

This contains notices and entries which adversely affect the land, e.g. charges, leases, easements and restrictive covenants.

Classes of title

(a) Freehold. Set out in s.9 of the LRA 2002

▪ **Absolute:** the best title 'virtually indefeasible and cannot be bettered' (Roper and Ruoff, *Law and Practice of Registered Conveyancing*, Sweet & Maxwell, 1991). Defined by s.9 as 'a person's title to the estate is such as a willing buyer could properly be advised by a competent professional adviser to accept'. Moreover, the Registrar may disregard the fact that the title is open to objection if of the opinion that the defect in the title will not cause the title to be disturbed. This continues the discretion of the Registrar which existed under the old law.

▪ **Possessory:** usually granted to a claimant by way of adverse possession. Section 9 provides that it can be granted where a person is in possession of the land, or of the rents and profits from it, and there is no other class of title with which he could be registered.

▪ **Qualified:** has the same effect as that of absolute, except that the title has been established only for a limited time or subject to reservations which cannot be disregarded using the discretion set out above under absolute title.

(b) Leasehold. Set out in s.10 of the LRA 2002

The rules are the same as for freehold except that there is an additional category of good title granted where the Registrar is satisfied as to the title granted to the lessee under the lease but not as to the title of the lessor.

▪ Scheme of the Act

The LRA 2002, like the LRA 1925, takes the different types of estates and interests in land dealt with above and classifies them for the purposes of land registration in the following ways:

▪ **Dispositions which must be completed by registration.**

▪ **Unregistered dispositions which override registered dispositions.** These correspond to the old category of overriding interests and the effect is that a buyer of the land can be bound by an interest that is not on the register. This is a highly significant area and often forms the subject of examination questions. We shall continue to refer to these as overriding interests.

▪ **Interests which do come within categories (a) or (b) and which must be protected by an entry against the title which they bind.** These were formerly known as minor interests and this term will continue to be used.

These categories will be explored in detail later but it is absolutely essential that you both know them and can apply them in an exam. Note that they do **not** apply to unregistered land! (See Chapter 3).

A thorough knowledge of the three ways in which the LRA 2002 classifies estates and interests in land will gain you marks in virtually all problem questions in the exam, not just questions specifically on land registration.

■Registrable dispositions

KEY STATUTORY PROVISION

Section 2(1) of the Land Registration Act 2002

If a disposition is required to be completed by registration, then it does not operate at law until it is registered in accordance with the requirements.

KEY DEFINITION

A **registrable disposition** is one that must be completed by registration.

- ■ **Transfer of the registered freehold estate.** This includes transfers by any of the following methods:
  - (a) For valuable or other consideration. (This does not include nominal consideration.)
  - (b) By way of gift.
  - (c) In pursuance of a court order.
  - (d) Transfer by personal representatives on death.
- ■ **The grant of a lease for more than seven years. In addition, certain leases for less than seven years are registrable, e.g. those which take effect more than three months after the date of the grant.**
- ■ **Certain other leases and rights arising under leases**, e.g. registration of the grant of a right to buy a lease under the Housing Act 1985.
- ■ **The express grant or reservation of legal easements, legal profits, legal rentcharges.**
- ■ **A first legal mortgage created out of the estate.** This will apply whenever existing legal mortgages are discharged and a new mortgage created. This rule has proved to be one of the main means of transferring land from the unregistered system to the registered system.

KEY STATUTORY PROVISION

Section 29 of the LRA 2002

The effect of a registered disposition is that it takes priority over any rights affecting the estate prior to the disposition which are not protected by registration. Thus an interest which is neither overriding nor protected by an entry on the register will not be binding on the purchaser.

There a few dispositions of freehold land or leases with at least seven years to run which will not be caught by the above rules and which will not need to be registered. An example is an assignment of a mortgage.

Voluntary registration is also possible, e.g. a freehold estate may be registered even though it is not being transferred.

■ Overriding interests

EXAM TIP

This is probably the most common topic on registered land for both essay questions and for problem questions.

KEY DEFINITION

An **overriding interest** is an unregistered disposition which overrides registered dispositions.

The LRA 2002 distinguishes between:

■ Interests which override on first registration of the land.
■ Interests which override on subsequent registration of the land.

Why?
This is because:

■ A registration of title for the first time may not be linked to a purchase, e.g. title can be registered voluntarily.
■ Therefore, the person who is the owner remains the same and so should be aware of what interests exist in the land.
■ The categories of overriding interests are wider than when land is subsequently registered. The reason is that this will be on a transfer of ownership.

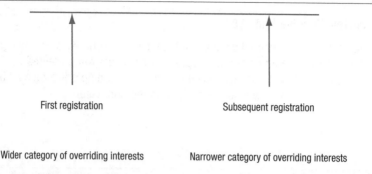

First registration

Subsequent registration

Wider category of overriding interests

Narrower category of overriding interests

EXAM TIP

If a problem question says that the title to land is registered and then asks you about e.g. the effect on third party rights of a sale, then this sale will result in a subsequent registration.

EXAM TIP

In an exam problem question you are faced with a particular right and you need to know what category it falls into. Check that you know what the three categories set out on page 25 mean and then check the right below.

Interests which override on first registration

- Leases not exceeding seven years.
- Interests of persons in actual occupation.
- Legal easements and profits (not equitable).
- Miscellaneous – e.g. local land charges.

Interests which override on subsequent registration

This will be the most important category in exams and so it is dealt with in much more detail.

Leases

- Legal leases for over seven years are registrable dispositions.

- Legal leases for less than this period are overriding interests.
- Equitable leases should be protected by registration as minor interests but, if they are not, then if the leaseholder is in actual occupation then they may have an overriding interest under LRA 2002, Sch.3, para. 2 (below).

Overriding interests of occupiers

KEY STATUTORY PROVISION

Schedule 3, para. 2 to the LRA 2002

'An interest belonging at the time of the disposition to a person in actual occupation ... except for –

(b) an interest of a person of whom enquiry was made before the disposition and who failed to disclose the right when he could reasonably have been expected to do so;

(c) an interest –
   (i) which belongs to a person whose occupation would not have been obvious on a reasonably careful inspection of the land at the time of the disposition, and
   (ii) of which the person to whom the disposition was made does not have actual knowledge at that time ...'

EXAM TIP

This is the most important exam tip of all! Schedule 3, para. 2 will come up somewhere in your exam either as:

- a direct question on land registration

or, for example:

- in a question on adverse possession
- in a question on leases.

FURTHER THINKING

The law changed from the LRA 1925 when the corresponding provision (s.70(1)(g) LRA 1925) did not provide that an overriding interest could be lost as in Sch. 3 para. 2(b) above. The new provision has in effect introduced the idea of notice found in unregistered land to registered land. This is controversial.

Check Chapter 1 and especially *Kingsnorth Finance* v. *Tizard* and compare the solution there with that in Sch.3, para. 2 above.

In a typical question based on *Williams & Glyn's Bank Ltd* v. *Boland* (1980) (see below) you should approach a problem question in this way:

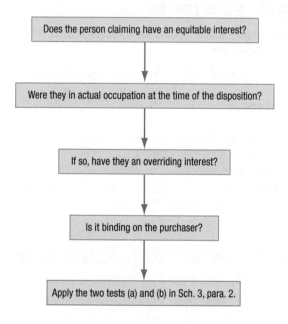

Does the person claiming have an equitable interest?

Were they in actual occupation at the time of the disposition?

If so, have they an overriding interest?

Is it binding on the purchaser?

Apply the two tests (a) and (b) in Sch. 3, para. 2.

The cases decided under the old law are still of use and establish the following principles:

KEY CASE

National Provincial Bank v. *Ainsworth* [1965] 2 All ER 472

Concerning: when does a right qualify for overriding status?

Legal principle

When it is an interest in land, whether it is legal or equitable.

Note: The facts of this case will not be relevant in an exam.

KEY CASE

Williams & Glyn's Bank v. *Boland* [1980] 2 All ER 408

Concerning: occupation of spouse giving an overriding interest

Facts

The wife had contributed to the purchase price of the property and so had acquired a beneficial interest in it. The husband mortgaged it to the bank, which sought possession when he did not keep up the repayments.

Legal principle

As the wife was in occupation under an equitable interest, she had an overriding interest which bound the bank.

The situation in this case and other similar ones can be seen in this way and you may find it useful to make a similar diagram when you get a problem question on this area:

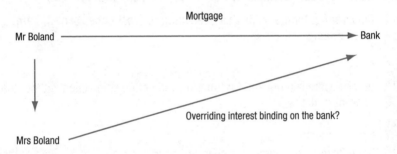

Mortgage

Mr Boland ⟶ Bank

Overriding interest binding on the bank?

Mrs Boland

Equitable interest? If so, is she also in occupation?

EXAM TIP

A problem question may ask you to discuss in more detail whether a person in Mrs Boland's position does have an equitable interest by applying the principles in *Lloyd's Bank* v. *Rosset* (1990).

REVISION NOTE

Check Chapter 5 and make sure that you are clear on the principles in *Rosset*.

KEY CASE

Chhokar v. *Chhokar* [1984] FLR 313

Concerning: can occupation be lost by temporary absence?

Facts

The wife, who had an equitable interest in the matrimonial home, was in hospital when her husband completed its sale.

Legal principle

She was still in occupation.

FURTHER THINKING

This is a common area for exam questions and the underlying principle is that of symbolic occupation. What if the clamant was away on a round-the-world trip which was to take two years?

KEY CASE

Abbey National Building Society v. *Cann* [1990] 1 All ER 1085

Concerning: time at which an overriding interest under Sch. 3, para. 2 takes effect

Facts

Carpets were laid out and furniture moved before completion without the consent of the seller.

Legal principle

In order to bind a purchaser, there must be occupation at the time of the disposition, i.e. completion. Here there were only acts preparatory to completion. In addition, where title is registered, the rights must remain subsisting at the time of registration.

FURTHER THINKING

The effect of this decision was to confine the principle in *Williams & Glyn's Bank* v. *Boland* (1980) to subsequent mortgages and was considered part of 'the retreat from *Boland*'. Another case which is said to be an example of this is *City of London Building Society* v. *Flegg* (1987): an overriding interest can be overreached.

REVISION NOTE

Check Chapter 1 for the principle of overreaching.

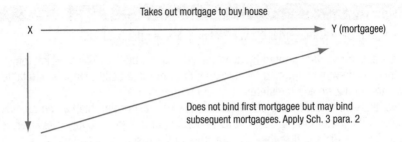

Takes out mortgage to buy house

X ──────────────────────────▶ Y (mortgagee)

Does not bind first mortgagee but may bind
subsequent mortgagees. Apply Sch. 3 para. 2

Z has an equitable interest + actual occupation = possible overriding interest

Problem area

Another way of explaining why a first mortgagee is not bound by the rights of a third party (Z) above is that Z has consented by implication to the mortgage – see e.g. *Paddington Building Society* v. *Mendelsohn* (1985).

Note also:

▌ *Hypo-Mortgage Services Ltd* v. *Robinson* (1997): a child cannot be in actual occupation. A useful discussion point in an essay question.

▌ *Ferrishurst Ltd* v. *Wallcite Ltd* (1999). This case held that an occupier need not be in occupation of the whole of the registered plot but this was reversed by Sch. 3, para. 2 of the LRA, which provides that an overriding interest extends only to land of which a person is in actual occupation.

Easements and profits

▌ New legal easements and profits created expressly (i.e. by deed) are registrable dispositions.

▌ Existing express legal easements and profits remain overriding.

▌ Equitable easements and profits are now minor interests.

▌ The only new legal easements and profits that can be overriding are those:
  – created by implied grant (rule in *Wheeldon* v. *Burrows* (1879) or s.62(1) LPA 1925).
  – created by prescription
    (Sch.3, para. 3, LRA 2002).

Where an easement can be overriding then it will be overriding in exactly the same cases as for rights of occupiers (above) (see Sch. 3, para. 3 LRA 2002) but there is one extra point to remember:

Where the person entitled to the easement or profit proves that it has been exercised in the year previous to the disposition then it will in effect always be overriding.

Example

X has a right of way (easement) over Y's land. Y sells the land to Z.

- If the easement was granted by deed then it will not bind Z unless registered.
- If the easement was granted by agreement but not in a deed then it is equitable and will not bind Z unless registered.
- If the easement was created by implied grant or prescription then it can be overriding but will not bind Z if the cases in Sch. 3 para. 3 above apply. However, it will bind Z if X exercised it in the year previous to the disposition (sale to Z).

REVISION NOTES

Check Chapter 1 and make sure that you know the rules on creation of an equitable interest by agreement.

Check Chapter 9 for easements created by implied grant and by prescription.

FURTHER THINKING

This whole area, and particularly overriding interests, is a very likely one for an essay question. Look at the Law Commission Papers for a start: Paper 254: *Land Registration for the 21st Century – A Consultative Document* (1998) and Paper 271: *Land Registration for the 21st Century – A Conveyancing Revolution* (2001). There are excellent accounts of the new law in e.g. Bogusz (2002) 65 MLR 556 and by Smith in L. Tee (ed.) *Land Law: Issues, Debates, Policy* (Willan Publishing, 2002), pp. 29–63.

Transitional provisions

- **Existing legal easements and profits** that are overriding remain so.
- **Existing leases for up to 21 years** remain overriding.
- Until October 2006 all legal easements and profits (even those created after the LRA 2002 came into force) remain overriding. This gives time to register them.
- **Interests which cease to be overriding in 2013**, e.g. a franchise (right to hold a market) and liability to repair the chancel of a church, will bind on first and subsequent registrations until that date.

See the interesting case of *Aston Cantlow PCC* v. *Wallbank* (2003), where the House of Lords rejected a claim that liability to repair the chancel of a church was in breach of the Human Rights Act 1998. The Parochial Church Council was not a public authority and, in any event, although it is an interference with property, the existence of such an overriding interest was not incompatible with the European Convention on Human Rights (ECHR).

Check Chapter 1 for details of the effect of the ECHR on Land Law.

Overriding interests which are abolished, i.e. do not override under either first or subsequent registration:

▮ Rights acquired or in the course of acquisition under the Limitation Acts – because of new rules for acquiring title here.

Check Chapter 6 and make sure that you understand and can apply the rules on acquisition of title by adverse possession.

▮ Equitable easements.

The existence of overriding interests has been criticised and you should be prepared for an essay question asking you whether they can be justified. The following reasons are put forward to justify their continued existence. Look at them and then read further to expand these points.

▮ They can easily be discovered by a purchaser. You need to analyse the rules in the LRA 2002 carefully here to arrive at your view.
▮ The value which is protected by the overriding interest is greater than the value of having all interests registered. For example, if the interest of a person in actual occupation was not overriding then it would be lost against a purchaser and in many cases the person with the interest does not know that they have it and so cannot register it. Yet if they had to register it, the consequence could be that they were made homeless.
▮ It is not worth putting some interests on the register. This is the argument for allowing leases for seven years or less to remain overriding. But is this argument going to be valid when we have electronic conveyancing?

▮ Protected registered interests: minor interests

Protected registered interests were formerly known as minor interests and this term will continue to be used here.

KEY DEFINITION

Protected registered interests are any interests which are not overriding and include: restrictive covenants; legal and equitable easements and profits; estate contract; and rights of beneficiaries under a trust.

These must be protected by an entry on the register to bind a purchaser. Note one significant change from the old law: where an interest is protected on the register by a notice then it cannot be an overriding interest (s.29(3) LRA). There are two ways in which an interest can be protected:

- **By a notice**. This can either be entered with the consent of the registered proprietor (RP) or unilaterally. If it is the latter then the RP can object and the Registrar decides the validity of the claim. Entry on the register does not mean that the interest is recognised by the law as valid; it simply means that it has priority over other interests. Certain interests cannot be protected by the entry of a notice: e.g. leases for less than three years and interests under a trust of land.
- **By a restriction**. This must be entered where two or more persons are registered as proprietors and the restriction ensures that interests capable of being overreached are in fact overreached. Thus interests under trusts of land cannot be protected by a notice as a restriction is more appropriate.

FURTHER THINKING

Consequences of a failure to register a minor interest
In *Peffer* v. *Rigg* (1978) two brothers-in-law purchased a house for their mother-in-law to live in. Only one of them was the RP but both had interests under a trust as they had contributed to the purchase price. These interests were not protected on the register. The RP later conveyed the property to his ex-wife for a nominal consideration and it was held that the ex-wife took subject to the rights of the beneficiaries as she was neither a purchaser for valuable consideration nor was she in good faith. This case is generally considered to be wrongly decided. It should be contrasted with *Midland Bank Trust Co. Ltd* v. *Green* (1981): see Chapter 3.

Note: The LRA 2002 also deals with the law on adverse possession, which is considered in Chapter 6.

■ Alteration of the register

This will not appear as a major issue in an exam, but you could mention it in an essay question on how the land registration system works. The rules on when the register can be altered are in s.65 and Sch.4, LRA 2002.

■Indemnities

The principle is that, if it turns out that the register needs to be altered, then compensation can be paid to whoever has suffered loss. The details are in s.103 and Sch. 8, LRA 2002.

Chapter summary
Putting it all together

TEST YOURSELF

☐ Can you tick all the points from the **revision checklist** at the beginning of this chapter?

☐ Take the **end-of-chapter quiz** on the companion website.

☐ Test your knowledge of the **key cases** with the **revision flashcards** on the website.

☐ Recall the legal principles of the **key cases** and **key statutory provisions** in this chapter.

☐ Attempt the **problem question** which was set out at the beginning of this chapter. See below for a final guide to it.

☐ Go to the companion website to test yourself on the **essay question** at the start of this chapter, and try out other questions.

Answer guidelines

See problem question at the start of the chapter.

Fred: Equitable profit – minor interest – needs to be protected by a notice on the register. If not, not binding.

Susie: Equitable lease: same as for Fred but if she had actually started to use the land she could claim that she had an overriding interest as a person in occupation under her equitable lease.

Jean – no right to register – just a personal right.

Elsie – may have an overriding interest as a person in actual occupation.

Making your answer stand out

▪ Good knowledge of the relevant case law especially in relation to Elsie.

▪ Spotting that, even if Elsie does have an overriding interest, John may not be bound by it – apply Sch 3, para. 2 LRA 2002.

3
Unregistered land

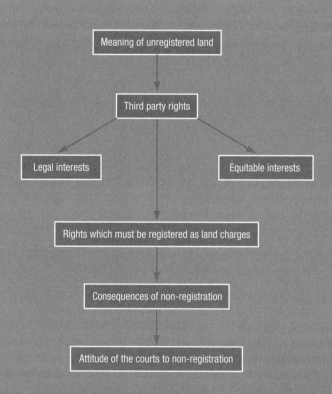

Meaning of unregistered land

Third party rights

Legal interests

Equitable interests

Rights which must be registered as land charges

Consequences of non-registration

Attitude of the courts to non-registration

Revision checklist

What you need to know:

☐ Difference between unregistered and registered land

☐ Which rights must be registered as land charges to bind a purchaser

☐ Effect of non-registration

☐ Which rights are not registrable as land charges

☐ Division of these rights into legal and equitable interests

☐ Are purchasers bound by legal interests which are not registrable as land charges?

☐ Are purchasers bound by equitable interests which are not registrable as land charges?

☐ Attitude of the courts when a right has not been registered as a land charge

Introduction
Understanding unregistered land

This topic needs to be looked at in conjunction with Chapter 2 on registered land, as many questions ask you to deal with a situation on the basis that title is either registered or unregistered. You must be able to go through each of the rights dealt with in this chapter and be able to identify:

▌ Does it need to be registered as a land charge or not?

▌ If not, whether it is legal or equitable and whether it can be binding on a purchaser. You will need to refer back to Chapter 1 on this.

Beware of the fact that there are three categories into which a right can fall. Make out a table for yourself with two columns: rights which must be registered as land charges and those which are not registrable. Subdivide the second column into two: legal interests and equitable interests and then go through all the rights and fit them into the correct column. It is the best way to learn them!

In short, this is a chapter where close attention to detail will pay particular dividends.

Essay question advice

An essay question could ask you to look at the extent to which rights in unregistered land need to be protected by entry on the land charges register and which rights depend for priority on the basic rules applicable to legal and equitable interests. A variation on this could be to ask you how important the doctrine of notice still is in unregistered land. Other possibilities are to ask for a comparison between the systems of registered and unregistered land or to ask about the extent to which the unregistered land system works in favour of purchasers.

Problem question advice

The obvious question is to give you a number of cases where third parties are claiming rights over land and to ask you if those rights have priority over a purchaser's rights. This will be a similar type of question to that for registered land. It is possible for a question to combine the two and ask you about the priority of third party rights on the assumption that title is either registered or unregistered.

For both essay and problem questions the message is clear: do not miss out unregistered land as a registered land question may also ask you about this area too.

Sample questions

Could you answer these questions? Have a look at the questions which follow. They are examples of a typical essay question and a typical problem question. This chapter will cover the issues raised in these questions and review the law necessary to provide a comprehensive answer. Guidelines on answering the problem question will be provided at the end of the chapter and guidelines on answering the essay question are on the companion website for this book.

Essay question

Although the property legislation of 1925 brought about a compromise between the rights of the purchaser of a legal estate and the rights of third parties, in fact the legislation favoured the purchaser.

Discuss this statement in relation to unregistered land.

Problem question

John has bought a freehold house with some farmland from Steve. Title was unregistered.

After John's purchase, Fred, Susie and Jean, who are all neighbours, come to see him with letters signed by Steve.

(a) Fred has a letter granting him the right to cut wood from trees on the land.

(b) Susie has a letter agreeing to grant her a two-year lease of one acre of the farmland, rent payable yearly. Susie has not started to use the land.

(c) Jean has a letter stating that she has a licence to park her caravan on the land.

In addition, Elsie, Steve's mother, arrives and says that she paid half the purchase price when Steve bought the house and so she has a right to stay there. Elsie was away on holiday when John purchased the house.

Advise John on whether he is bound by any of these claims.

REVISION NOTE

You should remember that this is the same problem which was set in Chapter 2 except that, there, title to the land was registered. When you have completed your answer to this question go back to Chapter 2 and compare your answers. An exam question may combine registered and unregistered land.

▉Meaning of unregistered land

This term simply means that the title to the land itself has not been registered, unlike in registered land. Therefore, when buying and selling the land it is necessary to rely on an examination of the title deeds to the property and make other enquiries rather than having the register to rely on.

However, this does not mean that there is no system of registration at all. Instead, some rights must be registered as land charges under the Land Charges Act 1972 but, as the actual title to the land is not registered, they are registered against the name of the estate owner, i.e. the owner of the legal estate of freehold or leasehold.

Do check that you understand this point and, above all, do not confuse registration of land charges with land registration itself.

▉Rights which must be registered as land charges

There are two crucial points about the land charges scheme which you must remember for your exam:

▉ A registered land charge is binding on a purchaser: the fact that a purchaser has no notice of it is irrelevant. The purchaser is expected to check the land charges register.

▉ If a land charge is not registered then it will not be binding on a purchaser, even if he/she does have notice.

Note: The legislation distinguishes between different types of purchase: see below.

To sum up: the only thing that matters is whether the right was registered as a land charge.

What rights must be registered as land charges?

Under the Land Charges Act 1925 (now the Land Charges Act 1972) a system was introduced under which the rights registrable as land charges are classified under headings A, B, C, D, E and F. They are set out in s.2 of the 1972 Act.

The ones to remember for the exam are:

Class C (i): puisne mortgage – i.e. a second or subsequent mortgage. These are legal mortgages which are not protected by the deposit of the title deeds to the property as the first mortgagee will have these. These are the only legal interests which are registrable as land charges.

Class C (iv): an estate contract. These include contracts to buy the fee simple and also contracts for a lease – equitable leases.

Class D (ii): a restrictive covenant entered into on or after 1 January 1926.

Class D (iii): an equitable easement created or arising on or after 1 January 1926.

You should learn the parts in italics very carefully.

In addition, the exam may require a knowledge of a *Class F Land Charge*. Under the Family Law Act 1996 spouses and (since the Civil Partnerships Act 2004) civil partners, have a personal right of occupation of the family home and this can be enforced against a purchaser if registered. Note that this is a personal right and does not give the spouse or civil partner an interest in the land.

■ Consequences of non-registration

<table>
<tr><td rowspan="1">KEY STATUTORY PROVISION</td><td>

Section 4 of the Land Charges Act 1972

Land charges in categories C (i), and F are void against a purchaser of any interests in the land.

Land charges in the other categories (C(iv), D(ii) and D(iii)) are void only against a purchaser for money or money's worth.

</td></tr>
</table>

<table>
<tr><td>KEY STATUTORY PROVISION</td><td>

Section199(1)(i) of the LPA 1925

If a right is not registered as a land charge when it should have been, then it is irrelevant that a purchaser has notice of it.

</td></tr>
</table>

Are legal and equitable interests in unregistered land binding on subsequent purchasers? A summary

EXAM TIP

This is vital for the exam! You must be absolutely clear for the exam:

- whether a right is registrable as a land charge;
- if not, then we return to the rules in Chapter 1 and ask whether it is:

(a) A legal interest? If so, it is binding on a purchaser automatically because 'legal interests bind the world'.
(b) An equitable interest? If so, whether it is binding on a purchaser depends on notice.

Go through the table below and make sure that you can remember where each right fits in. Unfortunately, this is just hard slog!

INTEREST	REGISTRABLE AS A LAND CHARGE?
LEGAL EASEMENTS AND PROFITS	NO: IT IS A LEGAL INTEREST AND BINDS A PURCHASER AUTOMATICALLY.
INTEREST OF A BENEFICIARY UNDER A TRUST	NO: IT IS AN EQUITABLE INTEREST AND SO WHETHER IT BINDS A PURCHASER DEPENDS ON NOTICE
EQUITABLE EASEMENTS AND PROFITS (POST-1926)	YES
EQUITABLE EASEMENTS AND PROFITS (PRE-1926)	NO: IT IS AN EQUITABLE INTEREST AND SO WHETHER IT BINDS A PURCHASER DEPENDS ON NOTICE
RESTRICTIVE COVENANTS (POST-1926)	YES
RESTRICTIVE COVENANTS (PRE-1926)	NO: IT IS AN EQUITABLE INTEREST AND SO WHETHER IT BINDS A PURCHASER DEPENDS ON NOTICE
ESTATE CONTRACTS	YES
PUISNE MORTGAGES. N.B. THESE ARE THE ONLY LEGAL INTERESTS IN THIS TABLE TO REQUIRE PROTECTION AS LAND CHARGES	YES

Midland Bank Trust Co. Ltd v. *Green* [1981] AC 513

Concerning: whether a failure to register a right as a land charge means that the courts will hold it void against a purchaser

Facts

A father granted his son an option to purchase his farm. This option should have been protected on the land charges register as a Class C (iv) land charge but was not. The father, in order to escape from the contract, sold the farm to his wife for only £550, purely to defeat the son's option, and it was held that the wife, as a purchaser, was not bound by it.

Legal principle

It is not fraud to rely on rights conferred by statute, i.e. the right to rely on the register, even if, as here, there may have been some element of bad faith.

FURTHER THINKING

Improve your exam marks by reading the judgment of Lord Wilberforce in the House of Lords and contrasting the approach of Denning MR in the Court of Appeal ([1979] 3 All ER 28), who argued that there was a constructive trust in favour of the son which bound the bank. Although Denning MR's argument failed, there are echoes of it in *Lloyd's Bank plc* v. *Carrick* (1996) (below).

REVISION NOTE

The argument that in some cases the courts may hold that a right can still bind a purchaser even though not registered did succeed in the registered land case of *Peffer* v. *Rigg* (1978) – see Chapter 2. Compare this with the above case and note the discussion in Chapter 2 on this point. Exam questions may link the position in unregistered and registered land.

The decision in *Midland Bank* v. *Green* dealt with rights which had been created by an estate contract. The case below was different:

▎ It was similar in that it concerned an estate contract.
▎ It was different because there was also an argument that the rights arose under a trust. Unlike an estate contract, rights under a trust do not come within any of the categories above of rights which have to be registered as land charges and whether they are binding on a purchaser depends on notice (see Chapter 1).

Lloyd's Bank v. *Carrick* [1996] 4 All ER 630

Concerning: whether, although an estate contract was not registered as a land charge, it could still bind a purchaser as the contract created a trust or, alternatively, an estoppel

Facts

A widow (Y) agreed to sell her house and buy a maisonette owned by her brother-in-law (X). Y paid the proceeds of sale of her house to X and moved into the maisonette, paying for substantial improvements to it. However, there was no conveyance of the property, nor was the agreement registered as a Class C (iv) land charge. X subsequently mortgaged the property to the bank.

Legal principle

Non-registration of the agreement made it void against the bank. In addition, Y claimed that she had a right under a trust due to her payment of the sale proceeds of her house to X and making the improvements. (See Chapter 5 and the principles in *Lloyd's Bank* v. *Rosset* (1990).) The court rejected this because her right arose from the contract and this excluded an independent right under a trust. Nor did her acts amount to an estoppel (see Chapter 8).

REVISION NOTES

Check that:

▌ You are familiar with registration of land charges (Chapter 3).
▌ You are familiar with the principles in *Lloyd's Bank* v. *Rosset* (Chapter 5).
▌ You are familiar with the conditions when an estoppel may apply (Chapter 8).

The situation in *Lloyds Bank* v. *Carrick* (1996) can be illustrated as follows:

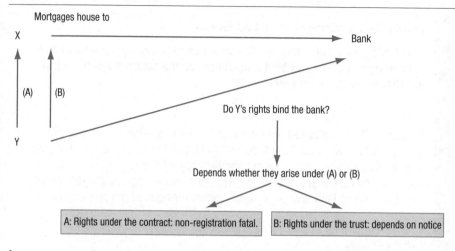

As you can see above, the court held that the rights depended on the contract.

Chapter summary
Putting it all together

☐ Can you tick all the points from the **revision checklist** at the beginning of this chapter?

☐ Take the **end-of-chapter quiz** on the companion website.

☐ Test your knowledge of the **key cases** with the **revision flashcards** on the website.

☐ Recall the legal principles of the **key cases** and **key statutory provisions** in this chapter.

☐ Attempt the **problem question** which was set out at the beginning of this chapter. See below for a final guide to it.

☐ Go to the companion website to test yourself on the **essay question** at the start of this chapter, and try out other questions.

Answer guidelines

See problem question at the start of the chapter.

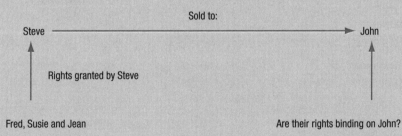

- Identify the rights: Fred = Profit; Susie = Lease; Jean = Licence; Elsie = right under a trust.
- Are they legal or equitable? Go back to the answer at the end of chapter 1.
- Do they need to be registered as land charges?
- Fred's profit – yes.
- Susie's equitable lease – yes – as an estate contract.
- Jean's licence – no – not a proprietary right.
- Elsie's right under a trust – no – so we fall back on the rules in Chapter 1 and give the same answer as we did then.

4
Co-ownership of land

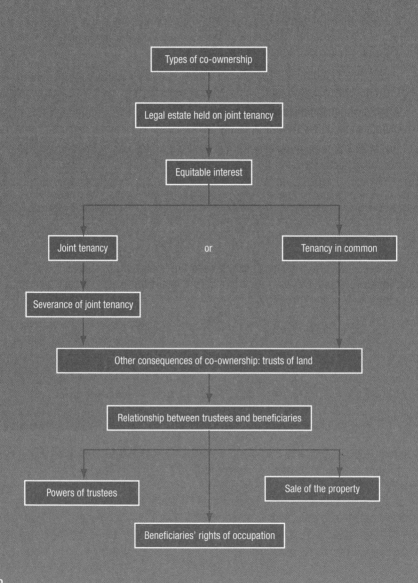

Revision checklist

What you need to know:

- [ ] Legal estate can only be held on a joint tenancy
- [ ] Equitable interests can be held on a joint tenancy or a tenancy in common
- [ ] Essential features of a joint tenancy
- [ ] Essential features of a tenancy in common
- [ ] Severance of a joint tenancy by statute
- [ ] Severance of a joint tenancy in equity
- [ ] Trust of land where there is co-ownership
- [ ] Powers of trustees of land
- [ ] Rights of beneficiaries to occupy
- [ ] Who can apply for sale of the land
- [ ] Principles on which the court orders a sale

Introduction
Understanding co-ownership of land

This area lends itself to problem questions and the issues are relatively straightforward. There are really no major recent cases but plenty of case law on applications for a sale of property.

Essay question

It is far more likely that you will get a problem question here, but a likely topic for an essay is a discussion of the law on trusts of land looking at the position of the trustees and the beneficiaries. You should be able to discuss the case law on powers of the court to order a sale and the link in *Bank of Baroda* v. *Dhillon* (1998) with overriding interests.

Problem question

This will require the ability to steer a clear path through attempts at severing a joint tenancy. There are a limited number of variations on the theme of how severance can take place and you must know them and be able to apply them.

It is common for a problem question then to go on to two other areas: the right of beneficiaries to occupy (check the original purpose for which the property was bought) and applications for a sale.

Sample question

In 2005 John, Mark, Conchetta and Louise were students at Melchester University and had won a prize on the lottery. They used their winnings to buy a house for them all to live in whilst they completed their studies. The purchase price was £100,000. John contributed £40,000 and the others each paid £20,000. They agreed that the house should belong to them equally and it was registered in the names of them all with a declaration that the survivor could give a receipt for capital money.

Later that year, John, having failed to submit an assignment on time, had to leave his course and so he sold his interest in the house to Alf, a fellow student.

Mark got married at Christmas and made a will leaving all his property to his wife, Florrie. They went on honeymoon to the seaside but Mark was drowned by a freak wave.

Louise told Conchetta that she could not stand living in the house just with her any more and that she wanted to sell her share. Conchetta was upset by this and a violent quarrel ensued. Louise then went to her solicitor and, acting on his advice, she sent a notice of severance by registered post to Conchetta. When the notice arrived, Conchetta was out and so Louise signed for it.

John and Louise now wish to sell the house but Conchetta and Alf wish to stay.

(a) Advise the parties on the devolution of the legal and equitable interests in the property.

(b) Advise Conchetta and Alf on whether they can remain in the house.

(c) Advise John and Louise on whether they can insist on a sale.

Types of co-ownership

This area deals with co-ownership of land. It is easily recognised in an exam question as there will be more than one legal owner. This is not an infallible guide to whether the problem is on co-ownership, but at the least you should check if it is!

There are three legal concepts which you need to master:

- Joint tenancy
- Tenancy in common
- Trusts of land

All of these will be involved in a problem question.

Legal estate held on joint tenancy

Where there is more than one owner of the legal estate then the legal estate must:

- Be held by the legal owners as joint tenants.

■ Be held by them on a trust of land.

Four unities are necessary for a joint tenancy to exist:

■ Time: the interests of all must vest at the same time.
■ Title: all must derive their title from the same document.
■ Interest: all must have the same interest.
■ Possession: all must be equally entitled to possession of the whole land.

Remember two vital points:

■ Co-owners cannot hold the legal estate as tenants in common.
■ The distinguishing feature of joint tenancy is the right of survivorship. This means that, as a joint tenant owns no individual share, then he cannot leave any part of his joint tenancy by will, nor does it pass under the intestacy rules. Instead, it passes to the surviving joint tenants. Section 184 of the LPA 1925 provides that where deaths occur in circumstances making it uncertain which died first then the younger shall be deemed to have survived the elder. (See *Hickman* v. *Peacey* (1945) – deaths in a bomb blast.)

Example

The legal estate to Blackacre is held by X and Y. This means that:

■ They are joint tenants.
■ There is a trust of land.

X dies. The legal estate automatically passes to Y.

Number of joint tenants:

KEY STATUTORY PROVISION	**Section 34(2) of the LPA 1925**
	Where land is conveyed to co-owners who are of full age then:
	■ they must be joint tenants;
	■ there cannot be more than four.

You often find that there are more than four persons named in the question. If so:

■ If they are all of full age, the first four take the legal estate but all of them can take a beneficial interest – see below.
■ If any of them are under 18, then they drop out and have only a beneficial interest.

■Equitable interest

Here there is a choice: it can be held on either:

■ Joint tenancy.
■ Tenancy in common.

Joint tenancy

This means that the right of survivorship applies to the beneficial interest.

Tenancy in common

This is the opposite of a joint tenancy. The only unity required is possession. Each is entitled to a separate share and can dispose of this share either during life or on death. Sometimes the four unities are present but there are words of severance (see below) and therefore there is a tenancy in common.

Remember that in a tenancy in common:

■ There are separate shares.
■ The right of survivorship does not apply.

Example

X and Y hold the legal estate to Blackacre on trust for themselves and Z.

■ The legal title must be held on a joint tenancy.
■ The equitable interest can be held on either: joint tenancy or tenancy in common.

If the equitable interest is held on a tenancy in common then X, Y and Z each have a separate share which they can sell or which can devolve on their death.

How do we tell if there is a joint tenancy or a tenancy in common?
The question may make it clear.

Example

X and Y agree that if they die then their interest in the property shall go to the other.

This agreement overrides anything else such as unequal contributions to the purchase price and there will be a joint tenancy as the parties intend that the right of survivorship shall apply.

The question may not make it clear and so you must look for:

Words of severance

Even if the four unities exist, there will not be a joint tenancy if there are words of severance, i.e. words which indicate that the parties are to hold separate shares. Examples are:

- 'in equal shares' – *Payne* v. *Webb* (1874).
- 'equally' – *Lewen* v. *Dodd* (1595).
- 'to be divided between' – *Peat* v. *Chapman* (1750).

Presumptions of equity

If there are no words of severance then look at this:

Equity leans against a joint tenancy and the law leans against a tenancy in common.

In the following cases equity presumes that there is a tenancy in common:

- Purchase in unequal shares – *Lake* v. *Gibson* (1729); *Bull* v. *Bull* (1955).
- Where there is a relationship of a commercial character e.g. partnership property – *Re Fuller's Contract* (1933).
- Where money is lent on mortgage by two or more persons they are presumed to hold the estate which they receive by way of security as tenants in common – *Morley* v. *Bird* (1798).

Remember: if there is an express agreement that the parties will hold as joint tenants, this will override any of the above presumptions.

EXAM TIP

Always refer to a joint tenant having an *interest* but a tenant in common having a *share*.

■ Severance of joint tenancy

Severance of an equitable joint tenancy to turn it into a tenancy in common

> **EXAM TIP**
>
> Problem questions frequently require you to look at this area. As a useful guide, the situation in the question usually involves a joint tenancy as it can be severed.

KEY STATUTORY PROVISION

Section 3(4) of the Administration of Estates Act 1925

Severance cannot be effected by will.

There are the following ways to sever a joint tenancy:

■ By notice in writing.
■ In equity.

By notice in writing

KEY STATUTORY PROVISION

Section 36(2) of the LPA 1925

A joint tenant may sever by giving notice of intention to sever to all other joint tenants.

Giving notice means serving notice (s.196(3) LPA 1925).

Re 88 Berkeley Road [1971] Ch 648

Concerning: service of a notice severing a joint tenancy

Facts

Both joint tenants (X and Y) occupied the same house and X served a notice on Y to sever which arrived at the house when X was there and therefore X signed for it.

Legal principle

As the notice had been served it was valid.

See also *Kinch* v. *Bullard* (1998).

In equity

KEY DEFINITION

Severance in equity means 'Such acts or things as would, in the case of personal estate, sever the tenancy in equity'. (Section 36(2) LPA 1925)

In *Williams* v. *Hensman* (1861) Page-Wood V-C said that there are three methods:

■ An act of any one of the parties operating on his own share, e.g. a sale of the joint tenant's beneficial interest or the bankruptcy of a joint tenant. In equity a sale will take place as soon as there is a specifically enforceable contract to sell.

Example

X sells his beneficial interest in Blackacre to W. This severs X's interest in equity and so W is a tenant in common. However, it does not affect X's legal estate which he continues to hold as a joint tenant.

■ Mutual agreement. In *Burgess* v. *Rawnsley* (1975) an oral agreement by one joint tenant to purchase the share of the other operated to sever even though the contract was not specifically enforceable as there was nothing in writing. In *Hunter* v. *Babbage* (1994) the couple were divorcing and made an unenforceable agreement to sever. The husband died before it could be formalised and it was held that the joint tenancy had been severed.

■ Any other course of dealing which shows that the interests of all were mutually treated as constituting a tenancy in common. In *Burgess* Sir John Pennycuick said that it includes negotiations which, although not resulting in an agreement, indicate a common intention to sever. Denning MR said that it included a course of dealing in which one party makes it clear to the others that he 'desires that their shares should no longer be held jointly but be held in common' but this is not considered to represent the law. Note that any agreement or common intention must be between all of the co-owners – a common examination point.

Note also: forfeiture.

If one joint tenant kills another, then the right of survivorship should not operate, as this would allow the murderer to benefit from their act.

Other consequences of co-ownership: trusts of land

Trusts of land

Once the question of who holds the legal title has been dealt with, one can then turn to the question of the terms on which it is held. The answer is that under the Trusts of Land and Appointment of Trustees Act 1996 (TLATA) a trust of land automatically comes into existence whenever the legal title to land is held by joint tenants (s.36(1) LPA, as amended by TLATA).

The following are the main provisions of TLATA and all references to sections are to sections of that Act.

EXAM TIP

In an exam, you will need to be able to apply these statutory provisions, although it is unlikely that a very detailed knowledge will be required. What is essential is that you know what area each section deals with and how they relate to each other.

Relationship between trustees and beneficiaries

Powers of trustees

Trustees have all the powers of an absolute owner of land (s.6(1)) but, as trustees, they are bound by the fiduciary duties of trustees when exercising their functions. As

Megarry V-C put it in *Cowan* v. *Scargill* (1984): 'they must put the interests of the beneficiaries first.'

KEY STATUTORY PROVISION

Section 6 of the TLATA 1996

Confers two specific powers on trustees:

(a) to purchase land by way of investment for the occupation of any beneficiary or for any other reason;

(b) to transfer the land to the beneficiaries when they are all of full age and capacity even though they have not requested this.

Exclusion and restriction of powers

KEY STATUTORY PROVISION

Section 8 of the TLATA 1996

Allows the settlor to exclude all or any of the provisions of s.6.

KEY STATUTORY PROVISION

Section 9 of the TLATA 1996

Provides that the trustees may, by power of attorney, delegate any of their functions relating to land to a beneficiary of full age and capacity.

Any delegation must be unanimous and therefore only one trustee can revoke it as this destroys unanimity. If trustees refuse to delegate, an application may be made to the court under s.14 TLATA 1996 by a beneficiary for an order that delegation should be made. Any delegate beneficiary has the same duties as an actual trustee.

Consultation with beneficiaries

KEY STATUTORY PROVISION

Section 11(1) of the TLATA 1996

'The trustees of land must –

(a) so far as practicable, consult the beneficiaries of full age who are beneficially entitled to an interest in possession of the land, and

(b) so far as is consistent with the general interest of the trust, give effect to these wishes of those beneficiaries, or (in cases of dispute) of the majority (according to the value of their combined interests).'

KEY STATUTORY PROVISION

Section 12 of the TLATA 1996

Gives a right of occupation to beneficiaries provided that the trust so allows but no right of occupation arises if the land is either unavailable or unsuitable for occupation by the beneficiary in question.

KEY STATUTORY PROVISION

Section 13 of the TLATA 1996

Allows the trustees power to exclude or restrict the right to occupy but the power must not be exercised unreasonably. Conditions may be imposed on occupation and s.13 sets out examples: paying outgoings and complying with obligations, e.g. ensuring that planning permission is complied with. Section 13 also sets out matters to which the trustees must have regard to when exercising their powers to restrict or exclude the right to occupy: intentions of the settlor; purposes for which the land is held on trust; and the circumstances and wishes of beneficiaries who would be entitled to occupy but for the exclusion or restriction.

■ Sale of property

Powers of the court to order a sale

These are contained in the following sections: s.14 deals with who can apply and s.15 with the principles on which the court can order a sale.

Section 14 of the TLATA 1996

KEY STATUTORY PROVISION

Allows any person interested in the trust to apply to the court for an order, which could be for, e.g. sale (see below), or authorising what would otherwise be a breach of trust. The term 'any person interested' includes trustees, beneficiaries, remaindermen and secured creditors of beneficiaries.

Section 15 of the TLATA 1996

KEY STATUTORY PROVISION

Sets out the following criteria to which the courts must have regard when settling disputes (in practice, and certainly in examination questions, these are particularly relevant when looking at disputes over whether land should be sold):

'(a) the intentions of the person or persons (if any) who created the trust,
(b) the purposes for which the property subject to the trust is held,
(c) the welfare of any minor who occupies, or might reasonably be expected to occupy any land subject to the trust as his home, and
(d) the interests of any secured creditor of any beneficiary.'

Mortgage Corporation Ltd v. *Shaire* [2001] 4 All ER 364

KEY CASE

Concerning: application of the principles in s.15 TLATA 1996

Facts

The house was held by X and Y as joint tenants. It was bought to provide a home for them and Y's son by a previous marriage. X owned a 25% share in equity and Y a 75% share. X mortgaged the house by forging Y's signature and after X's death the mortgagee sought a sale. The court refused.

Legal principle

By comparison with the previous law, Parliament had intended to 'tip the scales more in favour of families and against banks and other chargees' (Neuberger J). Nevertheless, the cases under the old law (s.30 LPA 1925) can still be referred to, albeit with caution.

The case does not establish an absolute principle that family rights come first: see e.g. *Pritchard Engelfield* v. *Steinberg* (2004), where the mortgagee did obtain a sale.

Bank of Baroda v. Dhillon (1998) 1 FCR 489

Concerning: relationship between s.15 TLATA and overriding interests

Facts

A bank applied for an order for sale of the matrimonial home.

Legal principle

This would be granted, even though the wife had an overriding interest under the LRA 1925 (now Sch. 3 para. 2 LRA 2002) which bound the bank. The crucial factor was that the children were grown up and after the sale W would still have enough money for other accommodation.

REVISION NOTE

Check your knowledge of overriding interests in Chapter 2.

An early case on s.30 LPA 1925, but which is probably still good law, is *Re Buchanan-Wollaston's Conveyance* (1939) where land was bought by co-owners to prevent it from being built on. One later wished to sell but the others did not. As the original purpose remained, the court refused to order a sale.

Read *Barca* v. *Mears* (2004) on the relationship between s.14 and s.15 TLATA 1996 and the Human Rights Act 1998 (ECHR – Article 8) – respect for private and family life.

Chapter summary
Putting it all together

- [ ] Can you tick all the points from the **revision checklist** at the beginning of this chapter?
- [ ] Take the **end-of-chapter quiz** on the companion website.
- [ ] Test your knowledge of the **key cases** with the **revision flashcards** on the website.
- [ ] Recall the legal principles of the **key cases** and **key statutory provisions** in this chapter.
- [ ] Attempt the **problem question** which was set out at the beginning of this chapter. See below for a final guide to it.
- [ ] Go to the companion website to test yourself on the **essay question** at the start of this chapter, and try out other questions.

Answer guidelines

See problem questions on page 52.
Note: JT = joint tenant
t/c = tenant in common
All references to sections below are to those in TLATA 1996.

Visual guide

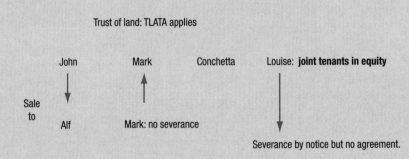

John   Mark   Conchetta   Louise: **joint tenants in law**

Trust of land: TLATA applies

John   Mark   Conchetta   Louise: **joint tenants in equity**

Sale
to

Alf   Mark: no severance

Severance by notice but no agreement.

John has severed: Alf a t/c.
At the end: John and Conchetta are left as legal JTs.
Alf, Conchetta and Louise are all t/c.

(a) Follow through the situation as above. Note that inequality of contributions does not make them t/c in equity, as their agreement plus the declaration at the Land Registry override this. Apply *Burgess* v. *Rawnsley* (1975) to the need for an agreement between Louise and Conchetta and *Re 88 Berkeley Road* (1971) to the receipt of the notice by Louise.

(b) Right to occupy: apply s.12 (also s.11 – need for consultation). If Alf has no right to occupy then s.13 – right can be restricted.

(c) Cannot insist on sale. Apply s.14 (right to apply) and s.15 (principles on which a sale can be ordered).

Making your answer stand out

▌ Mention of the possible application of the Human Rights Act.

▌ Link with overriding interests.

5
Trusts and the home

```
┌─────────────────────────┐
│   Situations where the  │
│  law of trusts is relevant │
└─────────────────────────┘
             │
             ▼
┌─────────────────────────┐
│ The law as it is: principles │
│   in Lloyds Bank v. Rosset   │
└─────────────────────────┘
        │           │
        ▼           ▼
┌──────────────┐  ┌──────────────┐
│ Common intention │ │ Direct contributions │
│ and detrimental  │ │              │
│     reliance     │ │              │
└──────────────┘  └──────────────┘
        │           │
        ▼           ▼
    ┌─────────────────────┐
    │    Size of the share │
    └─────────────────────┘
             │
             ▼
    ┌─────────────────────┐
    │  Possible relevance  │
    │     of estoppel      │
    └─────────────────────┘
             │
             ▼
    ┌─────────────────────┐
    │    Terminology in    │
    │      this area       │
    └─────────────────────┘
             │
             ▼
    ┌─────────────────────┐
    │ Giving effect to the │
    │ beneficial interest  │
    │      of a party      │
    └─────────────────────┘
             │
             ▼
    ┌─────────────────────┐
    │ The law as it ought  │
    │       to be?         │
    └─────────────────────┘
             │
             ▼
    ┌─────────────────────┐
    │ Where is the law in  │
    │  England going? Oxley │
    │ v. Hiscock: possible │
    │ statutory intervention │
    └─────────────────────┘
             │
             ▼
    ┌─────────────────────┐
    │  Approaches in Canada, │
    │ Australia and New Zealand │
    └─────────────────────┘
```

Revision checklist

What you need to know:

- [ ] When the law of trusts is relevant to disputes over the home
- [ ] Where the law is now
- [ ] Two ways of claiming:
  - claims based on common intention and detrimental reliance
  - claims based on direct financial contributions
- [ ] How the size of the share is determined
- [ ] Rights which an equitable interest gives
- [ ] Where the law should be going: approaches in other countries, possible changes in English law

Introduction
Understanding trusts and the home

This chapter deals with a familiar topic for examination questions: the part played by equity in disputes over the home. Unlike some other areas, this one is frequently met in practice and it is also a favourite of examiners. The fundamental principles are not difficult but students often, for some reason, fail to master them. It is most likely to feature as a problem question in a Land Law examination where it may well be linked with a point about land registration. It could also be an essay question. It is also an excellent topic to consider at this stage as it involves you in revising material covered in Chapters 1, 2, 3 and 4.

The law of trusts is relevant in situations where the parties are married or are cohabiting but also where, for example, parents contribute to the deposit on a house for their children and where a sister sells her house and goes to live with her brother and helps him pay off the mortgage on his house. There have been problems with the appropriate terminology to use in these cases: resulting trust, constructive trust or estoppel? For now, just concentrate on mastering the rules and we will look at the terminology towards the end of this chapter.

Essay question advice

This can be a topic in examination questions but much will depend on the extent to which this topic is taught in the Equity course. A general essay on, for example, constructive trusts, in an Equity exam will involve a discussion of this area. However, a Land Law exam may ask you to discuss the present state of the law in the light of, for instance, different approaches in other Commonwealth jurisdictions. You must first be absolutely clear what the present law is and then be able to evaluate possible future developments.

It is very easy to say that the present law is unjust. What is far less easy to arrive at is a coherent set of principles to replace it and to defend your ideas. The temptation here is to let the heart rule the head and to say, for example, that the decision in *Burns* v. *Burns* (1984) (below) was wrong and unjust because one is sympathetic to Mrs Burns. A really good answer will take the facts of a case like this and test other possible solutions against it. We will return to this point later.

Problem question advice

You are faced with a problem in the examination on this area. Look first at the facts and see if the parties are seeking a divorce or an order on the breakdown of a civil partnership. (Under the Civil Partnerships Act 2004 the court has the same powers to make orders on the breakdown of a registered civil partnership as it does on a divorce.) If so, then the law of property is not relevant and the matter comes under Family Law. Otherwise it is.

A problem question in the exam typically involves cohabitees but it need not do so. It can involve married partners where the issue is not distribution of assets on a divorce but, for example, where the house was mortgaged and the issue is the rights of one party to the marriage against the lender. Another possibility is where parents have contributed to the purchase of a house which is in the name of their children. Once you have decided that a party does have a beneficial interest, you must go on to look at the rules for deciding the respective shares.

In addition, and this is where a problem question in Land Law is likely to differ from one on this area in an Equity exam, the question may also ask you to decide if, assuming that a party does have a beneficial interest in the land, that interest is binding on a purchaser. This will involve considering if title to the land is registered or not and the rules on, for example, overriding interests. You will need to link the material in this chapter with those in Chapters 2 and 3 and also refer back to Chapter 1 where there is an equitable interest in unregistered land. You may also need to use the detail in Chapter 4 on the rights contained in TLATA 1996 of beneficiaries and others in land held on trust.

To sum up: there may be two issues:

(a) Does a party acquire a beneficial interest and, if so, what are the rules on its size?
(b) Assuming that they do have a beneficial interest, is it binding on a purchaser?

▌Sample questions

Could you answer these questions? Have a look at the questions which follow. They are examples of a typical essay question and a typical problem question. This chapter will cover the issues raised in these questions and review the law necessary to provide a comprehensive answer. Guidelines on answering the problem question will be provided at the end of the chapter and guidelines on answering the essay question are on the companion website for this book. You should note that the problem question is probably longer than you might find in the exam, as a last section has been included asking you about the position if title to the house was unregistered. This is to make sure that you recall the difference between registered and unregistered land.

Essay question

'For more than a generation it has been widely argued that the law regulating the proprietary rights of those living in non-marital relationships is unsatisfactory.'

(Rotherham (2004) 68 Conv 268)

Do you agree?

Problem question

Robert and Josephine met in 2000 and decided to set up home together. They bought 'The Laurels', a registered freehold property, for £300,000 with the aid of a mortgage of £100,000 from the Friendly Building Society secured by a legal charge over the property. Josephine was registered as sole proprietor, as Robert's earnings as a proofreader fluctuated greatly. Robert contributed 5% of the deposit from his savings but Josephine paid the rest and she initially assumed responsibility for the mortgage repayments.

In 2002 Robert said to Josephine: 'I realise what a financial drain these payments must be to you. From now on, I will pay all the utility bills so that your earnings are used for the mortgage repayments.' Josephine replied: 'It's about time that you contributed to our joint venture.' Robert, feeling guilty after Josephine's words, then started to begin work on an extension to the house to give them extra room when their family arrived.

In 2004 Josephine needed money to expand a business venture of hers and so, whilst Robert was on a six-month expedition to Tibet, she took out loan from the Newtown Bank secured by a second legal charge on 'The Laurels'.

In 2006 Josephine met Terry and told Robert that their relationship was at an end and that he must leave 'The Laurels'.

Advise Robert what rights, if any, he has in respect of 'The Laurels'.
Would it make any difference to your answer if title to 'The Laurels' was unregistered?

■ The law of trusts and the family home

You need to be aware of the following statutory provisions:

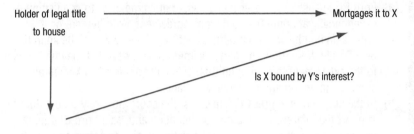

Holder of legal title to house

Mortgages it to X

Is X bound by Y's interest?

Y has a beneficial interest in the property

EXAM TIP

In any problem question you need to point out, near the start of your answer, the relevance of the statutory provisions on the creation of trusts of land.

Section 53(1)(b) of the LPA 1925

Declaration of a trust of land must be in writing or there must be written evidence of it.

Section 53(2) of the LPA 1925

The requirement in s.53(1)(b) does not apply to resulting, implied or constructive trusts. (This is why trusts of the kind discussed below are not affected by the need for writing.)

Lloyds Bank v. Rosset [1991] 1 All ER 111

Concerning: principles to be applied when deciding if a person has a beneficial interest in the home

Legal principles

(a) Lord Bridge asked whether there was, at any time prior to acquisition or exceptionally at some later date, any agreement, arrangement or understanding between the parties that the property was to be shared beneficially. If so, then the party claiming must show that they have acted to their detriment in relying on this. This category is often known as common intention and detrimental reliance.

(b) In the absence of express discussions, the court must rely on conduct to support the inference of a common intention and, said Lord Bridge, in nearly every case the only relevant conduct is direct contributions to the purchase price. It was, he said, extremely doubtful if anything else will do. This category is often known as direct contribution.

EXAM TIP

The *Rosset* principles are absolutely vital, especially when tackling a problem question. Learn them carefully and apply each of them separately to the situation. For some reason, students often link them together and confuse the issue.

■ Common intention and detrimental reliance

Hammond v. Mitchell [1991] 2 All ER 109

Concerning: acquisition of a beneficial interest in the home under the common intention and detrimental reliance head

Facts

The house was in the man's name but he told his partner that this was for tax reasons and he said to her: 'Don't worry about the future because when we are married it will be half yours anyway.' She relied on this to her detriment by, for example, helping him in his business.

Legal principle

A common intention which is relied on to the detriment of the party claiming is capable of giving a beneficial interest in property.

How clear does the common intention have to be? In this case, the man indicated to the woman that the house was to be half hers but there is no evidence that she agreed. How, then, can intention be common? But in *Springette* v. *Defoe* (1992) it was held that the parties must at least communicate: it is no good just saying afterwards that they both had the same intention if they never communicated this to each other.

FURTHER THINKING

The requirement to find a common intention has often been criticised: the reality is that people do not usually discuss these matters when property is acquired as they do not anticipate their relationship coming to an end. See two articles: Clarke, 'The Family Home, Intention and Agreement' (1992) Fam Law 72. and Gardner, 'Rethinking Family Property' (1993) 109 LQR 263. The article by Gardner is an excellent survey of the whole area.

■ Direct contributions

KEY CASE

Buggs v. *Buggs* [2003] EWHC 1538 (Ch)

Concerning: relevance of direct contributions

Facts

X sought a declaration that she was entitled to a share in a flat which had been bought for the mother of her former husband.

Legal principle

Although X had undoubtedly made a direct contribution to the cost of acquisition it was clear that the intention had been that the whole family unit would benefit from the investment in the flat and not X personally.

KEY CASE

Burns v. *Burns* [1984] 1 All ER 244

Concerning: where there is neither evidence of an agreement showing common intention nor direct contributions

Facts

The claimant had lived with the defendant for 17 years. They were not married and the house was in the name of him (the defendant). The claimant had not made any direct contribution to the cost of acquisition nor was there evidence of any common intention that the claimant should have a beneficial share.

Legal principle

Where there is no evidence of a common intention about beneficial ownership nor direct contributions then there is no entitlement to a beneficial share.

▌ Although this case predates *Rosset*, the law prior to *Rosset* was developing on the lines put forward by Lord Bridge (see above).
▌ When the present law is criticised (see below) it is usually because of decisions of this kind.

EXAM TIP

It is very easy to say that Valerie Burns in this case was treated unfairly but you will get marks for suggesting reasonable alternatives to the present law (see below).

Size of the share

EXAM TIP

Make sure that you deal with this completely separately from the preceding question of whether a party has a beneficial interest at all. Do not confuse the two!

Oxley v. Hiscock [2004] EWCA Civ 546, [2004] 3 All ER 703

Concerning: principles to be applied in determining the size of the share of a beneficial interest

Facts

The essential point was that the home was in the name of Mr Hiscock but both he and Mrs Oxley had made substantial contributions to the cost of its acquisition. There was no problem in deciding that Mrs Oxley had a beneficial interest – the question was its size.

Legal principle

Chadwick LJ in the Court of Appeal proposed that the test should be the simple one of what 'would be a fair share for each party having regard to the whole course of dealing between them in relation to the property?'

This case seems to have changed the law from what it was thought to be after *Midland Bank* v. *Cooke* (1995). Here the Court of Appeal held that the court must undertake a survey of the whole course of dealing between the parties relevant to their ownership and occupation of the property to determine 'what proportions the parties must have been assumed to have intended (from the outset) for their beneficial ownership'. Chadwick LJ in *Oxley* found this test unsatisfactory.

■ Possible relevance of estoppel

Estoppel can be relevant in other areas and Chapter 8 deals with it in more detail. A definition which is repeated here is:

Estoppel arises where one person (the representee) has been led to act on the representation of another (the representor). If so, and if the representee then acts to their detriment on the basis of this promise, then in equity the court may grant them a remedy.

REVISION NOTE

Look at Chapter 8 and make sure that you understand the definition of estoppel.

The courts have sometimes used the concept of estoppel on its own in family homes cases although at other times it has been linked to the constructive trust – see above. An example of estoppel is *Pascoe* v. *Turner* (1979).

In cases of estoppel, the courts have always had discretion over what remedy to award. Compare with the discussion above in *Oxley* v. *Hiscock*.

EXAM TIP

Estoppel will not usually arise as a completely separate issue in typical problem questions on the family home and it is often linked to the *Rosset* principle called 'common intention and detrimental reliance'. However, note a recent case where estoppel was pleaded and failed: *H* v. *M* (2004).

■ Terminology in this area

In giving effect to their decisions the courts have used the concepts of:

■ resulting or implied trust;
■ constructive trust;
■ estoppel, which has been linked with the imposition of a constructive trust in e.g. *Lloyds Bank* v. *Rosset* (1990).

The courts have often observed that it matters little, if at all, whether the trust which is imposed is called a resulting, implied or a constructive trust (see e.g. Lord Diplock in *Gissing* v. *Gissing* (1970)). However, the fundamental difference between a resulting and a constructive trust in this context is that if a resulting trust is held to have arisen when a party is claiming on the basis of contributions, then the extent of their beneficial share will be in proportion to their contributions. If a constructive trust is imposed, then the courts have a wider discretion as to the extent of the shares.

It is interesting that in *Oxley* v. *Hiscock* (2004) Chadwick LJ, when discussing the law on ascertaining the extent of the beneficial interests (see above), used estoppel language.

■ Giving effect to the beneficial interest of a party

In a problem question it will do no harm to round off an answer by pointing out that as this is Equity, the beneficial interest will be held on a tenancy in common unless there is a specific intention to hold as joint tenants.

REVISION NOTE

Check the distinction between a joint tenancy and a tenant in common in Chapter 4.

■ The law as it ought to be?

A problem question would not use the case below but, if you are being asked to think more widely in an essay question, then a knowledge of the approaches of the Court of

Appeal in the 1970s and, in particular, that of Lord Denning, can add to your marks. This case is a good example of his approach.

Eves v. *Eves* [1975] 2 All ER 768

Concerning: deciding if a party has a beneficial interest

Facts

The claimant, aged 19, lived with the defendant who told her that, although the house was to be for themselves and their children, it would have to be put into his name only as the claimant was under 21. This untrue statement was, he later admitted, simply just an excuse to avoid putting it into joint names.

The claimant did not pay anything towards the cost of acquisition but she did a great deal of work on it by, for example, wielding a 14lb sledgehammer to break up concrete and in general renovating what was a dilapidated house.

Legal principle

Denning MR in the Court of Appeal held that, having regard to the defendant's conduct at the time in telling the claimant that it was to be their joint home, it would be inequitable to allow him to deny her a share in the house. He quoted his judgment in *Cooke* v. *Head* (1972): 'Whenever two parties by their joint efforts acquire property for their joint benefit, the court may impose or impute a constructive or resulting trust.'

■ Where is the law in England going? *Oxley* v. *Hiscock*: possible statutory intervention

■ *Oxley* v. *Hiscock* – the emphasis seems to be very much on quantification of the beneficial interests rather than whether a party gets an interest at all as in *Burns* v. *Burns* (1984).

■ Statutory intervention – note the Law Commission Paper *Sharing Homes* (2002): this failed to come up with a workable statutory solution and was thought to be disappointing. The Civil Partnerships Act 2004 has extended statutory intervention to those in registered same-sex relationships so there will be increased pressure to extend this to those in opposite-sex relationships who are not married.

■ The Law Commission has just issued a consultation paper (no. 179) which proposes a new system for dealing with disputes between cohabitees over the home and other property. The starting point would be economic advantage gained and economic disadvantage suffered by the parties to the relationship.

■Approaches in Canada, Australia and New Zealand

EXAM TIP

You will boost your marks by knowledge of the position in other jurisdictions. The articles by Gardner (above) and Rotherham (2004) Conv 68 will give you enough information for most answers. Remember that, where information is concerned, as distinct from ideas, Gardner is less satisfactory, as it appeared so some years ago.

FURTHER THINKING

Main cases in other jurisdictions:
Canada: based on unjust enrichment – see *Pettkus* v. *Becker* (1980) and *Peter* v. *Beblow* (1991).
Australia: based on unconscionability – see *Baumgartner* v. *Baumgartner* (1987).
New Zealand: was based on meeting the reasonable expectations of the parties – see *Gillies* v. *Keogh* (1989) – but is it now? Look at Rotherham's article (above).

Take any of these cases and ask yourself: would the decision have been different under the *Rosset* principles?

Chapter summary
Putting it all together

☐ Can you tick all the points from the **revision checklist** at the beginning of this chapter?

☐ Take the **end-of-chapter quiz** on the companion website.

☐ Test your knowledge of the **key cases** with the **revision flashcards** on the website.

☐ Recall the legal principles of the **key cases** and **key statutory provisions** in this chapter.

☐ Attempt the **problem question** which was set out at the beginning of this chapter. See below for a final guide to it.

☐ Go to the companion website to test yourself on the **essay question** at the start of this chapter, and try out other questions.

Answer guidelines

See the problem question on page 68.

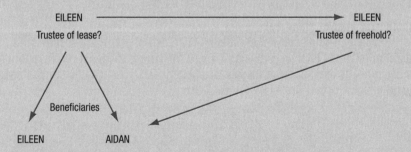

First look at whether Robert has a beneficial interest. Parties are not married – nor is there any express declaration of trust to satisfy s.53(1)(b) LPA 1925 – so Robert's claim must be under a resulting/constructive trust and/or estoppel.

Rosset principles:

(a) A direct contribution at the time of acquisition – also evidence that Josephine intended that he should contribute – bought the property to set up home together.

(b) Common intention – not clear what was actually said – court cannot attribute intention – *Springette* v. *Defoe* – but may have been discussions – if so, did

Robert act on them to his detriment – also building of extension seems a response to what was said.

Not clear if Robert will be able to establish a beneficial interest in equity but may be able to do so. Therefore, press on to consider:

▌ Size of the share. Most recent authority is *Oxley* v. *Hiscock*.
▌ Therefore, Robert may be a tenant in common in equity of 'The Laurels' and entitled to a share in the proceeds of sale.

Now deal with whether Robert's rights are binding on:

(a) The first mortgagee – Friendly Building Society. No – he gets no interest in the property until completion: *Abbey National Building Society* v. *Cann* (1990) and *Paddington Building Society* v. *Mendelsohn* (1985).
(b) The second mortgagee – Newtown Bank. This is a post-acquisition mortgage, so Robert's interest may be binding if it overrides that of the bank. Apply Sch. 3, para. 2 LRA 2002 and note that Robert's absence may not deprive him of his interest – *Chhokar* v. *Chhokar* (see Chapter 2).

If Robert's interest does bind the bank, then Robert does have a right to occupy under s.12 of TLATA but the bank could still apply for a sale – apply s.14 of TLATA and the criteria in s.15 together with *Bank of Baroda* v. *Dhillon* (1998) (see Chapter 4).

If title was unregistered, then answer (a) above would be the same, but as far as the Newtown Bank is concerned Robert's equitable interest would be binding on it if the bank had notice – *Kingsnorth Trust Ltd* v. *Tizard* (1986) – interests under trusts are not registrable as land charges (see Chapters 1 and 2).

Making your answer stand out
Clear knowledge and discussion of different approaches, e.g. in the section on quantification of the interest. Although *Oxley* v. *Hiscock* is the most recent authority, you could briefly mention what the law was before. This area is so fluid that it can change again!

6
Adverse possession

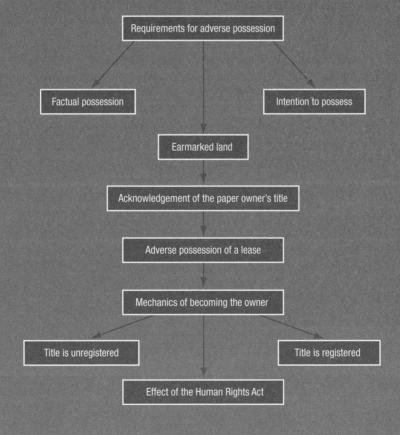

Requirements for adverse possession

Factual possession

Intention to possess

Earmarked land

Acknowledgement of the paper owner's title

Adverse possession of a lease

Mechanics of becoming the owner

Title is unregistered

Title is registered

Effect of the Human Rights Act

Revision checklist

What you need to know:

- [ ] Meaning of factual possession
- [ ] Meaning of intention to possess
- [ ] Distinction between these ideas
- [ ] Relevance of an acknowledgement of the owner's title
- [ ] Significance of the land being earmarked
- [ ] Mechanics of acquiring title: unregistered land
- [ ] Mechanics of acquiring title: registered land
- [ ] Different rules where a lease is adversely possessed
- [ ] Impact of the Human Rights Act

Introduction
Understanding adverse possession

This topic is not difficult and often appears in exams. The key is to go through all the stages in how title is acquired by adverse possession, logically, paying particular attention to:

- The effect of the decision in *Pye* v. *Graham* (2002) – this is a really vital recent case which is relevant to a number of areas: factual possession, intention to possess, possible acknowledgement of the owner's title and the effect of the Human Rights Act 1998.
- The mechanics of acquiring title under the LRA 2002: the stages are quite detailed, although not difficult in themselves, and can figure prominently in both essay and problem questions.
- The position where a lease rather than a freehold is adversely possessed.

Essay question advice

There are two obvious areas for an essay question, which overlap to some extent:

- A comparison between the methods of acquiring title where title to land is unregistered with where it is registered.
- The impact of the Human Rights Act. This is where a good knowledge of *Pye* v. *Graham* (2002) is essential.

You can boost your marks by looking at newspaper accounts of *Pye* v. *Graham* (this case was widely reported in the national press) where the papers referred to other cases where land had been adversely possessed. This will help in painting a picture of the social context of the subject.

Problem question advice

A problem question will almost certainly involve most of the areas in this chapter: the extent to which the land has been adversely possessed; the possible effect of an acknowledgement of the owner's title (marks to be gained here by appreciating that the law is not entirely clear); earmarking of the land for future use; and the actual application for registration.

Do *not* start your answer until you have checked:

- Dates: make a note of when possession began and the date now.
- Is it a claim to a freehold or to a leasehold?
- Is title to the land registered or unregistered? As always in Land Law, do check if the question asks in the alternative: on the basis that title is registered or unregistered.

Sample questions

Could you answer these questions? Have a look at the questions which follow. They are examples of a typical essay question and a typical problem question. This chapter will cover the issues raised in these questions and review the law necessary to provide a comprehensive answer. Guidelines on answering the problem question will be provided at the end of the chapter and guidelines on answering the essay question are on the companion website for this book.

Essay question

Do you consider that the changes made by the Land Registration Act 2002 to acquisition of title to registered land by adverse possession have made the system fairer, especially by comparison with the position where title is unregistered?

Problem question

In 1995 Amy started to cultivate a field behind her house. She planted vegetables and later she erected a shed to store her gardening tools. Later on she also planted a hedge along the boundary to act as a windbreak. The registered owner of the field was Robert, who lived in France.

On a day visit to inspect his property, Robert told Amy that he had no present use for the field but that he intended at some future time to seek planning permission to build on it. Meanwhile he told Amy that he would be prepared to grant her a short lease. Amy told him to write to her solicitor about this but, although negotiations followed, no lease was ever granted.

Amy died in 1999, leaving all her property to her son Christopher, who had lived with her. Robert also died in 2004, leaving all his property to his daughter Sally. Sally has been in poor health and lives in a nursing home.

It is now 2007 and Christopher asks your advice on whether he can be registered as owner of the field and, if so, on the procedures which will apply.

The actual periods for which land must be adversely possessed will be explained in detail at the end of this chapter but it will help you to understand this topic if you remember the following basic times:

- Registered land: initially 10 years.
- Unregistered land: 12 years.

■Factual possession

These words from the judgment of Slade J in *Powell* v. *McFarlane* (1977) were accepted by the House of Lords in *Pye* v. *Graham* (2002) as representing the law: 'Factual possession signifies an appropriate degree of physical control ... Everything must depend on the particular circumstances but broadly, I think what must be shown ... is that the alleged possessor has been dealing with the land as an occupying owner might have been expected to deal with it and that no one else has done so.'

KEY CASE	*Williams* v. *Usherwood* [1983] 45 P & CR 235
	Concerning: factual possession
	Facts
	Land was enclosed by a fence, three cars were parked on it and a driveway was paved.
	Legal principle
	This was sufficient factual possession.

Pye (JA) (Oxford) Ltd v. *Graham* **[2002] UKHL 30, [2002] 3 All ER 865**

Concerning: factual possession

Facts

The defendants had farmed land, including grazing cattle, maintaining the boundary and trimming the hedges and re-seeding the land. Also the paper owner had no key to the gate to the land.

Legal principle

This was sufficient factual possession.

There are many cases where there was no factual possession. Select one to contrast with the above cases, e.g. *Tecbild Ltd* v. *Chamberlain* (1969), where the playing on the land by children and the tethering of ponies was not enough.

EXAM TIP

Rather than learn many cases on what constitutes factual possession, it is better to be clear about what Slade J said (above) in *Pye* v. *Graham* and apply this to the question.

■ Intention to possess

You need to deal with this separately from factual possession, as it may be that, although there is factual possession, there is clearly no intention to possess.

Example

X is in occupation of a locked house, which he has agreed to look after for a friend whilst the friend is away on holiday. He may have factual possession but he does not intend to actually possess it.

This example is from the judgment of Lord Browne-Wilkinson in *Pye* v. *Graham*, in which he emphasised that intention to own is not required, only intention to possess. This means that the alleged possessor (AP) does not have to prove that he believed that the land was his (he knows that it is not his anyway) but that he intended to exclude the paper owner.

Earmarked land

This follows from the above point. Can an AP intend to possess where he is aware that the paper owner had intended future use? It follows that he can, as it is sufficient if he intends to exclude the paper owner. The present law is now clear and easily recognised in exams. It is illustrated by the case below.

KEY CASE

Buckinghamshire County Council v. *Moran* [1989] 2 All ER 225

Concerning: whether a claim to adverse possession can be defeated by showing that the paper owner had intended a future use for it

Facts

The defendant enclosed land belonging to the claimant and treated it as an extension of his garden. The claimant had intended to use the land to carry out a road diversion.

Legal principle

The fact that the paper owner had a future intended use for the land for a road diversion did not stop the defendant adversely possessing it.

FURTHER THINKING

Although the law on earmarking now appears settled, this was not always so and you can add marks to your answer by referring to how the law reached its present position. Earlier cases had held that earmarking land for a future use could prevent adverse possession until the intended use for the land was abandoned. Look at *Leigh* v. *Jack* (1879) and also at the judgment of Denning MR in *Wallis's Cayton Bay Holiday Camp Ltd.* v. *Shell-Mex and BP Ltd* (1974). The latest important case in this area is *Pye* v. *Graham* (2002) (above) where the House of Lords held that it would only be very occasionally that the fact that there is an intended future use will prevent adverse possession.

Acknowledgement of the paper owner's title

This point often arises in exam questions and is easily recognised.

Example

X has occupied a house belonging to Y for the past nine years and has treated it as his own. Y then says to X that he owes rent for the use of the house. An exam situation may say that either:

- X says that he will pay rent to Y.
- X actually pays rent to Y and becomes Y's tenant.

In the second situation, X is clearly no longer an adverse possessor, as he has become Y's tenant. It is impossible to be both at the same time, otherwise all tenants would claim ownership by adverse possession.

It is the first example which has caused difficulty.

Pye (JA) (Oxford) Ltd v. *Graham* [2002] UKHL 30, [2002] 3 All ER 865

Concerning: whether willingness of the squatter to pay if asked defeats a claim to adverse possession

Facts

The defendant (the AP) occupied fields owned by the claimant (the paper owner) under a licence and when this expired they asked for a further licence which the paper owners refused to grant. The defendants remained in occupation.

Legal principle

Lord Browne-Wilkinson held that 'there is no inconsistency between a squatter being willing to pay the paper owner if asked and his being in the meantime in possession'. This follows from the earlier point that an intention to own is not required. If it was, willingness to pay would be fatal to a claim, as why should I pay someone else for what I claim to own?

Adverse possession of a lease

This presents a different problem in one way, although the basic requirements for adverse possession remain.

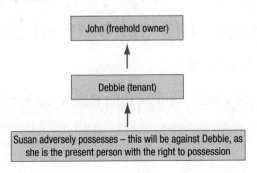

John (freehold owner)

↑

Debbie (tenant)

↑

Susan adversely possesses – this will be against Debbie, as she is the present person with the right to possession

The position differs depending on whether title to the land is registered or unregistered:

Unregistered

■ If Susan adversely possesses, then she has the right to possession but this does not end Debbie's lease: so Debbie remains liable on the lease.

■ If Debbie breaches the covenants in the lease then John may claim to forfeit it. This will then give John the immediate right to possession and so he can then eject Susan.

■ If he fails to do this then she may, on the expiry of a further 12 years, claim John's freehold. (Time does not begin to run against John until the lease expires.)

■ John can also bring forward the time when he can bring possession proceedings to evict Susan by taking a surrender of the lease from Debbie (*Fairweather* v. *St Marylebone Property Co. Ltd* (1962)).

Registered

There will be a transfer of the lease as the squatter can be registered as owner of it. Meanwhile, it appears that it will be possible before the squatter is registered for the landlord to take a surrender of the lease under the principles in *Fairweather* (above).

FURTHER THINKING

The decision in *Fairweather* v. *St Marylebone* has been controversial, although is now firmly entrenched in the law. The point is simple: how can the tenant surrender the lease when he no longer has it for practical purposes as the squatter has possession now? Look at Wade (1962) 78 LQR 541.

■Applications to be registered as proprietor: the scheme of the LRA 2002 (Sch.6)

Note: By contrast with the old law, the new scheme has a number of safeguards for the existing proprietor. In a problem question you will first need to establish that there is a right to be registered, as this is not affected by the LRA 2002. Only after you have dealt with this should you go through the procedures under this scheme.

Note the abbreviations:
AP = adverse possessor
RP = registered proprietor

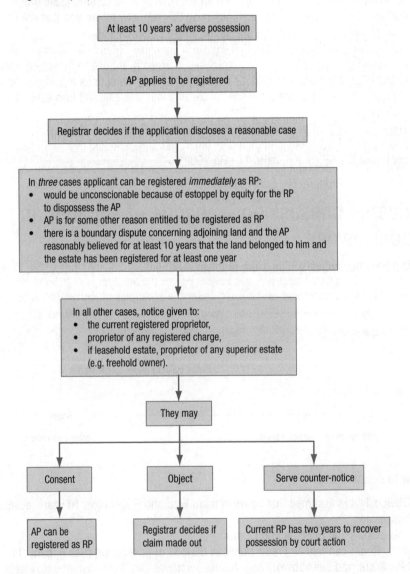

Summary of the above scheme

The effect is that, except in three special cases, the current RP has two years from the date on which she is informed of the claim of the AP to recover possession.

Note the following extra points, which could crop up in the exam as side issues:

▌ No application can be made when the current RP is unable, because of mental disability, either to make decisions on an application or to communicate those decisions. Exam questions sometimes raise this issue by telling you that the RP is ill or abroad. This is irrelevant unless the above exceptions apply.

▌ The AP takes subject to all existing legal and equitable rights in the land except registered charges. This is why a registered chargee is entitled to be served with notice of an application so that it can object. The only exceptions are where the AP is registered in one of the three special cases above. Here he will take subject to the charge.

▌ The AP can rely on periods of possession by another AP – e.g. X adversely possesses for five years and then dies but Y, her son, who had lived with her, continues the AP (Sch.6, para. 11 LRA 2002).

Adverse possession – change of squatter and paper owner

This point often appears in an exam problem question:

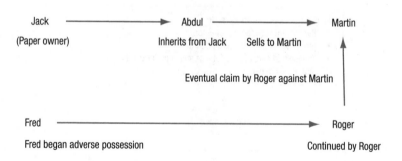

How to deal with this:

▌ Obviously it is assumed that between them Fred and Roger have 10 years' adverse possession.
▌ This possession must be continuous.
▌ If so, Roger can rely on Fred's previous periods of possession (Sch.6, para. 11 LRA 2002, and see above).
▌ Abdul is a donee.
▌ He is bound by any rights in the land and this includes rights in the course of being acquired by adverse possession – often known (although not strictly) as a mini-fee simple.

▌ Roger is a purchaser.

▌ Any rights in the course of being acquired by adverse possession count as overriding interests under Sch.3, para. 2 LRA 2002 so the question is whether Roger is actually bound – would the occupation have been obvious on a reasonably careful inspection? Did Roger fail to disclose it when he could have been reasonably expected to?

REVISION NOTE

Check overriding interests under Sch.3, para. 2 LRA 2002 (see Chapter 2): it is absolutely vital that you apply this point!

▌Applications to be registered as proprietor: unregistered land

The position is simple: when the period of 12 years is completed, the AP becomes entitled to be the owner. There is no actual process as such but the AP will need to prove to whomever he sells that he is indeed the owner. He takes the land subject to all existing rights.

FURTHER THINKING

You should be prepared for an essay question on the justification for the law on adverse possession. Read Dockray (1985) Conv 272, who looks at the justifications for allowing acquisition by adverse possession and then at the Law Commission Paper 254, *Land Registration for the 21st Century* paras. 10.5–10.9. You should then link this with the discussion on the effect of the Human Rights Act on this area of the law (below).

▌Effect of the Human Rights Act 1998

In *Pye* v. *Graham* (2002) the European Court of Human Rights held that the provisions on acquiring title by adverse possession to unregistered land were in breach of Article 1, Protocol I of the Convention. This was, of course, because of lack of safeguards for the paper owner.

REVISION NOTE

Check Chapter 1 to make sure that you know the effect of Article 1, Protocol I.

Chapter summary
Putting it all together

Answer guidelines

See problem question on page 82.

Visual guide

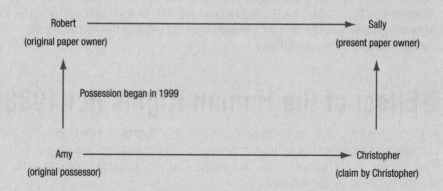

- Begin by checking dates and if title registered: it is, so initial period of ten years and here it is now 2007 and Amy's possession began in 1995.
- Now check whether Amy had factual possession and intention to possess for this

time: look carefully at facts and compare with cases. May be doubtful if she has, but assume that she has and press on.

▌ Significance of negotiations for lease: note *Pye* v. *Graham.*
▌ Deal with relevance of earmarking.
▌ Christopher takes over Amy's claim (Sch. 6, para. 11, LRA 2002).
▌ Sally inherits the land (s.28, LRA 2002).
▌ Sally's health (Sch. 6, para. 8(2), LRA 2002).
▌ Application for registration (procedures in Sch.6, LRA 2002).

Making your answer stand out

Mention the possible impact of the Human Rights Act 1998 – see *Pye* v. *Graham* (2002). The Act may not actually affect the claim as here title is registered, but a brief mention will show that you can think about wider issues.

7
Leases

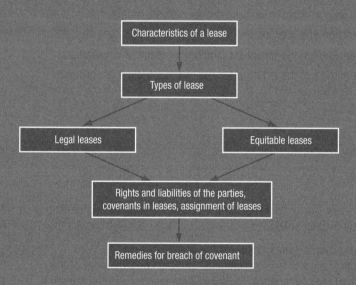

Characteristics of a lease

↓

Types of lease

↓

Legal leases   Equitable leases

↓

Rights and liabilities of the parties,
covenants in leases, assignment of leases

↓

Remedies for breach of covenant

Revision checklist

What you need to know:

- [ ] Essential characteristics of a lease
- [ ] Distinction between a lease and a licence
- [ ] Main types of leases
- [ ] Distinction between a legal and an equitable lease
- [ ] Extent to which legal leases are binding on a transferee of the land
- [ ] Extent to which equitable leases are binding on a transferee of the land
- [ ] Distinction between express and implied covenants in leases
- [ ] Main examples of implied covenants
- [ ] When a landlord can refuse consent to an assignment of a lease
- [ ] When covenants in leases bind successors in title
- [ ] Position of a subtenant
- [ ] Remedies of the tenant for landlord's breach of covenants
- [ ] Remedies of the landlord for the tenant's breach of covenants

Introduction
Understanding leases

This is usually the longest topic in the Land Law syllabus and questions can involve three fairly distinct areas:

- Whether a lease exists at all – is it a licence instead?
- Whether a lease is legal or equitable and the consequences of this.
- Breach of the covenants in the lease, who is liable and the remedies.

Essay question advice

A very common essay question is to ask you if it matters whether a lease is legal or equitable. The answer is of course that it does and you then need to explore this. This question is a bit hackneyed now and you could get a more challenging question on:

(a) The lease/licence distinction.
(b) The rules on the running of covenants in leases.

Problem questions often ask you to deal with liability for breach of covenants. This is a good area to score marks, as there are lots of issues and also lots of complex points for the good candidate to score extra marks on. On the other hand, all reasonably prepared candidates should be able to find enough material for a reasonable pass.

You should tackle such a problem question as follows:

(a) Has there been a breach of covenant?
(b) If so, what is the date of the lease and is it legal or equitable? (See below for why these points are vital.)
(c) Who is liable on the covenants?
(d) Can a purchaser of the freehold reversion sue on them?
(e) If there is liability, what are the remedies?

Other examples of problem questions are:

(a) The lease/licence distinction, possibly linked with what type of lease it is, assuming that it is a lease at all.
(b) Whether a lease is binding on a purchaser of the freehold. This could be linked with the question in (a) above.

Sample questions

Could you answer these questions? Have a look at the questions which follow. They are examples of a typical essay question and a typical problem question. This chapter will cover the issues raised in these questions and review the law necessary to provide a comprehensive answer. Guidelines on answering the problem question will be provided at the end of the chapter and guidelines on answering the essay question are on the companion website for this book.

'There is no distinction between a lease ... and an agreement for a lease.'

(*Re Maughan* (1885)).

Do you consider that this is an accurate statement of the law as it is today?

Fiona has just purchased 155 High Street, Hanbury, a freehold registered property, consisting of a house and an adjoining office, from Terry. Fiona asks your advice on the following matters:

(a) The top floor of the house is occupied by Ted under an agreement made two years ago where he is allowed to stay for five years paying rent at £300 a quarter. The agreement is unsigned and it provides that the owner of the house agrees to clean Ted's premises and retains a duplicate key to enable them to enter in order to do this. Ted tells Fiona that Terry never cleaned the premises and that Ted never wanted him to do so.

(b) The office is occupied by Josephine under a seven-year legal lease granted last year at a rent of £6,000 a year, payable quarterly. The lease contains the following covenants:

(i) That Josephine will keep the premises in good repair.

(ii) That the permitted use of the premises is a high class retail shop.

(iii) That the lease cannot be assigned without the consent of the landlord.

(iv) That in the event of any breach of covenant the landlord may forfeit the lease.

Josephine now wishes to assign the lease to Eileen, who wishes to open a travel agency. Fiona has discovered that the premises have not been kept in repair.

Advise Fiona on her rights and obligations.

■ Characteristics of a lease

KEY DEFINITIONS

A **lease** is an estate in the land which therefore gives a proprietary interest in the land. It must be distinguished from a **licence**, which only gives a personal right in the land. Although the fact that licences only create personal interests has proved controversial in the past, it is the law today.

REVISION NOTE

Go to Chapter 1 and revise leases as legal estates in the land and as equitable interests in the land.

Keep in mind two vital consequences of the right being a lease and not a licence:

■ It can bind third parties, e.g. purchasers of the freehold.

■ The holder of a lease has security of tenure created by statute but a licensee has not.

Note terminology: the parties to a lease are the landlord and the tenant but they are legally the lessor (landlord) and the lessee (tenant).

You will not be required to know the details of the statutory protection given to tenants in a Land Law exam unless your syllabus expressly includes landlord and tenant law.

The essential characteristics of a lease were set out in this case:

KEY CASE

Street v. *Mountford* [1985] 2 All ER 289

Concerning: essential characteristics of a lease

Facts

Under what was described as a licence agreement, X was given exclusive possession of furnished rooms at a rent. She had signed a statement at the end of the agreement that this was not intended to give rise to a tenancy under the Rent Acts. It was held that in fact she did have a tenancy.

Legal principle

A lease must have three characteristics:

▌ exclusive possession,
▌ for a fixed or periodic term,
▌ at a rent.

If so, there will be a tenancy unless there are exceptional circumstances which make it a licence.

The fact that the agreement is described as a licence does not prevent it being a lease if the above characteristics are present. The only intention of the parties which is relevant is the intention to grant exclusive possession.

EXAM TIP

The principles in this case are absolutely vital for a problem question on the lease/licence distinction.

There have been many cases which have applied the principles in *Street* v. *Mountford*. Here are three of them:

KEY CASE

Antoniades v. *Villiers* [1988] 3 All ER 1058

Concerning: whether 'separate' licence agreements were in fact a lease

Facts

A couple entered into two separate but identical agreements under which they were given the right to occupy rooms and each had separate responsibility for payment of half the rent. The agreement provided that they were to use the rooms either in common with the owner or with other licensees permitted by him.

Legal principle

Despite the attempt to make this look like two separate licence agreements, it was in fact a lease. A vital point was that they had the choice of either two single beds or one double bed. They chose a double bed and so clearly they intended to occupy the rooms jointly.

KEY CASE

AG Securities v. *Vaughan* [1988] 3 All ER 1058

Concerning: separate licence agreements

Facts

Four men signed separate agreements, described as licences. They were signed on different days and the payments were different. The agreements said that the occupants did not have exclusive possession.

Legal principle

Where it is clear on the facts, as here, that there is no intention that the occupants should have exclusive possession then there is not a lease. Unlike in *Antoniades* (above), there was no connection between the different occupants.

KEY CASE

Aslan v. *Murphy* [1990] 1 WLR 766

Concerning: 'sham agreements'

Facts

The occupier was required to vacate the premises for 90 minutes each day and the owner retained the key. The actual situation indicated that there was a lease. The court disregarded both of the above facts.

Legal principle

What matters are the three characteristics in *Street* v. *Mountford*. Here there was a lease.

The rule that a lease must be for a term certain is illustrated by *Prudential Assurance Co. Ltd* v. *London Residuary Body* (1992): lease granted until a road required for road widening invalid.

Leases are also classified by the length of time they last for and the main types to learn for an exam are:

■ Leases for a fixed term.
■ Periodic tenancies.

Periodic tenancies often arise in exam questions and it is vital to be able to recognise them: they arise from payment of rent at periodic intervals.

Example

X agrees to let Y rent a flat, rent to be payable monthly. This is a monthly periodic tenancy. They are referred to again below.

■Types of lease

Legal leases

A lease will be legal if created by deed but there is an important exception:

KEY STATUTORY PROVISION

Section 54(2) of the LPA 1925

A lease not exceeding three years can be legal without any formalities (it can even be oral) if:

■ in possession;
■ best rent – commercial rent;
■ no fine – no premium.

Equitable leases

A lease can be equitable under the principle in *Walsh* v. *Lonsdale* (1882) as an agreement for a lease but it must satisfy the three requirements for a valid agreement set out in s.2 of the Law of Property (Miscellaneous Provisions) Act 1989.

REVISION NOTE
Check Chapter 1 to make sure that you understand and can apply these requirements.

KEY CASE

***Walsh* v. *Lonsdale* [1882] 21 Ch D 9**

Concerning: creation of equitable leases

Facts

A lease was granted but not by deed. Thus it was only equitable. An agreement for a lease can be enforced by equity on the basis of the maxim that 'equity looks on that as done which ought to be done', i.e. if a person has agreed to grant a lease then they ought to do so and, as far as possible, equity will assume that they have done so.

Legal principle

An agreement for a lease can create a valid equitable lease.

Comparison between legal and equitable leases

A very common essay question asks if there are any differences between legal and equitable leases.

Legal leases	Equitable leases
Created by deed except for leases not exceeding three years.	Created by agreement which satisfies s.2 Law of Property (Miscellaneous Provisions) Act 1989.
Not granted at the discretion of the court.	Granted at the discretion of the court – equitable remedies are discretionary.
Tenant under a legal lease can claim implied easements under s.62(1) LPA 1925.	Tenant under an equitable lease cannot claim implied easements under s.62(1) LPA 1925 – equitable lease is not a conveyance.

In addition, there are different rules on whether legal and equitable leases can bind third parties (see below).

Leases and third parties

Here is a summary:

Registered land:

- Legal leases for over seven years are registrable dispositions.
- Legal leases for less than this period are overriding interests.
- Equitable leases should be registered but, if they are not, then if the leaseholder is in actual occupation then they may have an overriding interest under Sch.3, para. 2 (see Chapter 2).

Unregistered land:

- Legal leases are binding on all third parties.
- Equitable leases need to be protected on the register of land charges as estate contracts: Class C (iv).

■Rights and liabilities of the parties, covenants in leases, assignment of leases

This area, together with remedies for breach of covenant, often forms a problem question in an exam. The situation can be set out like this:

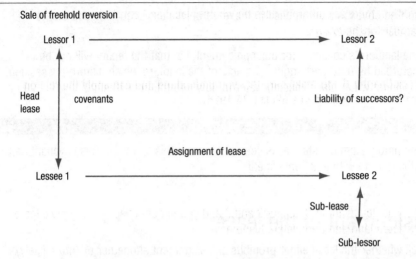

Sale of freehold reversion

Lessor 1 ──────────────────────────► Lessor 2

Head lease | covenants | Liability of successors?

Assignment of lease

Lessee 1 ──────────────────────────► Lessee 2

Sub-lease

Sub-lessor

EXAM TIP

The first point to check in a problem question is the date when the lease was granted: if it was on or after 1 January 1996, your answer will differ from if it was before this date as the Landlord and Tenant (Covenants) Act 1995 will apply. The actual changes are explained below.

Take each of these areas:

Covenants in the head lease

Distinguish between:

■ Express covenants – i.e. actually contained in the lease.
■ Implied covenants – i.e. implied by law.

KEY DEFINITION

Covenants: promises in a deed.

Even where the lease is equitable (i.e. no deed), it is usual to talk of covenants.

Typical examples of covenants in an exam question are: repairing, payment of rent, that the tenant will only use the premises for certain purposes. Exam questions will normally set these out as express covenants.

Implied covenants are implied in the lease unless excluded – a good one to remember for the exam is:

▮ The landlord's covenant for quiet enjoyment, i.e. that the tenant will not be disturbed by third party rights and acts of the landlord which disturb possession, e.g. burst water pipes causing water to flow into the premises.

EXAM TIP

A common exam question asks you about noise: this is a trap! This covenant has nothing to do with quiet enjoyment.

Assignment of the lease

Check whether the lease either prohibits an assignment altogether or (more likely) allows assignment provided that the landlord consents.

KEY STATUTORY PROVISION

Section 19(1) of the Landlord and Tenant Act 1927

The landlord must not withhold consent unreasonably.

Be prepared for a question asking you to discuss a refusal of consent.

KEY CASE

International Drilling Fluids Ltd v. *Louisville Investments (Uxbridge) Ltd* [1986] 1 All ER 321

Concerning: refusal by landlord of consent to an assignment of a lease

Legal principle

The landlord is entitled to be protected from having the premises used or occupied in an undesirable way by an undesirable assignee (or tenant) but consent to an assignment cannot be refused on grounds which have nothing to do with the relationship of landlord and tenant. So a personal dislike would not be enough.

Section 1(3) of the Landlord and Tenant Act 1988

If the tenant asks for consent in writing, the landlord must give or refuse it in writing and must do this in a reasonable time.

Liabilities of the original landlord and tenant on the covenants

Distinguish between pre-1 January 1996 and post-1 January 1996 leases:

▮ If the lease was granted before 1 January 1996 then both landlord and tenant remain liable on the covenants for the whole term of the lease even if they are no longer parties i.e. the tenant has assigned the lease and the landlord has sold the freehold reversion.

▮ If the lease was granted on or after 1 January 1996 then the Landlord and Tenant (Covenants) Act 1995 applies (note: all the references to sections below are to sections of this Act).
  – Section 5 – the tenant on assigning the lease is released from his covenants.
  – However, the landlord may, as a condition of agreeing to the assignment, require the tenant to enter into an authorised guarantee agreement (AGA) (s.16) guaranteeing that the incoming tenant will perform the covenants. This works like this:

EXAMPLE

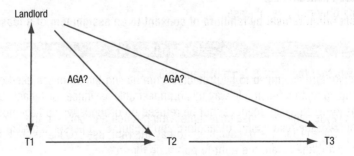

When the landlord gives consent to the assignment from T1 to T2 he can require T1 to enter an AGA under which T1 guarantees T2's liabilities under the lease. When T2 assigns to T3 the landlord may require T2 to enter into an AGA but, when the assignment is complete, T1's liability ends. This is a common exam point.

Section 6 of the Landlord and Tenant (Covenants) Act 1995

The landlord may, on selling the freehold reversion, be released from liability on his covenants. The procedure is set out in s.8.

Liabilities of incoming landlords and tenants on the covenants

Once again, it is necessary to distinguish between pre-1 January 1996 and post-1 January 1996 situations:

Landlord 1 ⟶ Landlord 2

Tenant 1 ⟶ Tenant 2

Pre-1996:
Remember the basic rules:
Covenants only run in legal leases.

EXAM TIP
Check whether the lease is legal or equitable.

Tenant 2 (T2) is liable on those covenants 'which touch and concern the land' (*Spencer's Case* (1583)), e.g. covenants to pay the rent, use covenants, but not a covenant giving the tenant the right to purchase the freehold.

Landlord 2 is liable to T2 under s.142 LPA 1925 and can enforce covenants against Tenant 1 and Tenant 2 which 'have reference to the subject matter of the lease' (s.141 LPA 1925). This term means fundamentally the same as the common law term 'touch and concern'.

The rules apply to both legal and equitable leases.

The fundamental rule is that both incoming landlords and tenants are bound by covenants unless they are 'personal in character'. This is very similar to the old 'touch and concern' test.

Post 1996:

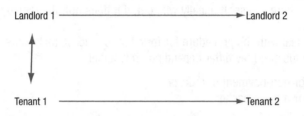

The rules apply to both legal and equitable leases.

Sub-leases

Remember three points:

■ In the old phrase, there is no 'privity of estate' between the landlord under the head lease and the subtenant' (ST), i.e. the landlord (L) is not a party to the sub-lease. This means that the landlord and the ST cannot directly enforce covenants against each other.

■ The landlord can, as an exception to the above rule, enforce a restrictive covenant which is negative by an injunction against the ST.

■ The landlord can sue the tenant under the head lease.

Example

There are two covenants in a lease:

(a) To repair the premises.

(b) Not to use the premises for any purpose other than a high-class grocer's shop.

T has sub-let to ST. L can enforce covenant (b) against ST as it is a negative restrictive covenant but can only enforce covenant (a) against T as this is a positive covenant.

REVISION NOTE

Check Chapter 10 for the rules on restrictive covenants.

▮ Remedies for breach of covenant

A problem question on breaches of covenant will usually also ask you what remedies the landlord has. This is often linked to a problem on breach of covenant and liability.

Remedies:

(a) Damages against the tenant.
(b) Claim to forfeit the lease.

Questions usually require you to discuss forfeiture, so always check that the lease contains a forfeiture clause. It usually will, but, if it does not, the remedy of forfeiture is not available.

When you deal with the procedure for forfeiture of a lease make sure you know what the grounds are: they differ depending on whether:

▮ forfeiture for non-payment of rent; *or*
▮ forfeiture for other breaches.

Procedure:

L issues formal demand for rent unless the lease provides that is not required.

Where breach is other than non-payment of rent, a notice is served under s.146 of the LPA 1925: this gives the tenant the opportunity to seek relief against forfeiture.

Where the breach is non-payment of rent the tenant can claim relief on certain conditions – pays arrears and landlord's costs and the court feels it just to grant relief.

Note: *Expert Clothing Ltd* v. *Hillgate House Ltd* (1987): Slade LJ said that the principle in deciding to grant relief from forfeiture is: is the breach capable of remedy?

Chapter summary
Putting it all together

☐ Can you tick all the points from the **revision checklist** at the beginning of this chapter?

☐ Take the **end-of-chapter quiz** on the companion website.

☐ Test your knowledge of the **key cases** with the **revision flashcards** on the website.

☐ Recall the legal principles of the **key cases** and **key statutory provisions** in this chapter.

☐ Attempt the **problem question** which was set out at the beginning of this chapter. See below for a final guide to it.

☐ Go to the companion website to test yourself on the **essay question** at the start of this chapter, and try out other questions.

Answer guidelines

See problem question at the start of the chapter.

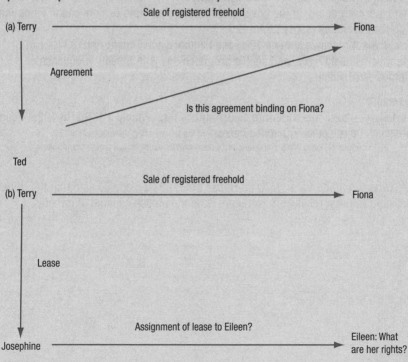

(a) Terry —— Sale of registered freehold ——→ Fiona

Agreement

Is this agreement binding on Fiona?

Ted

(b) Terry —— Sale of registered freehold ——→ Fiona

Lease

Assignment of lease to Eileen?

Josephine ——————————→ Eileen: What are her rights?

(a) Lease or licence?

Look at the three tests:

▌ Exclusive possession?
▌ Payment of rent?
▌ Intention to create relationship of landlord and tenant?

If it could be a lease, is it for a definite term?

Could be either a lease or a licence so:

If a licence, not binding on Terry.

If a lease, may bind Terry but first check:

What type of lease is it? Legal leases for more than three years should be created by deed (s.54(2) LPA 1925). Is it an equitable lease? Apply *Walsh* v. *Lonsdale* and the requirements in s.2 Law of Property (Miscellaneous Provisions) Act 1989.

If equitable, does it bind Terry? Title is registered, so agreement could have been registered but does not seem to have been.

However, may be a legal periodical quarterly lease as rent has been paid. If so, will count as an overriding interest (lease for less than seven years) and will bind Terry.

(b) Lease is legal and was entered into after 1 January 1996 so the Landlord and Tenants (Covenants) Act 1996 will apply.

Is there a breach of any of the covenants? Yes – repair and use covenant. Fiona may sue on the covenants: s.141 LPA 1925.

Assignment of lease: apply s.19 of the Landlord and Tenant Act 1927 – can consent be withheld? Yes, as Eileen's proposed use is in breach of covenant.

Remedies of Fiona:

▌ Damages.
▌ Forfeiture – lease has forfeiture clause: procedure – apply s.146 LPA 1925 – can breaches be remedied? Discuss cases.

8
Licences and estoppel

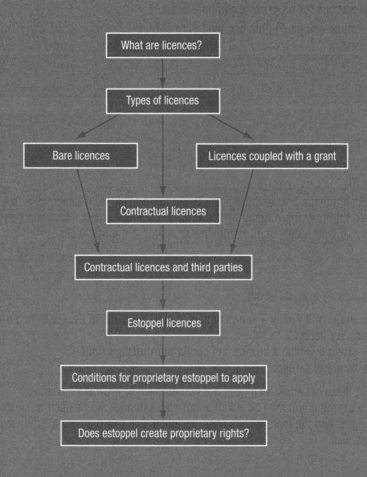

What are licences?

Types of licences

Bare licences

Licences coupled with a grant

Contractual licences

Contractual licences and third parties

Estoppel licences

Conditions for proprietary estoppel to apply

Does estoppel create proprietary rights?

Revision checklist

What you need to know:

- [ ] Licences as personal rights
- [ ] Distinction between licences and property rights
- [ ] What is a bare licence?
- [ ] What is a contractual licence?
- [ ] What is a licence coupled with a grant?
- [ ] Do contractual licences create interests in land?
- [ ] When proprietary estoppel can create a licence
- [ ] Conditions for proprietary estoppel to apply
- [ ] Whether estoppel rights can bind third parties

Introduction
Understanding licences and estoppel

This is not a difficult area and you should aim to do really well. Unlike other parts of Land Law, there are more cases here and fewer technical points. However, you do need to have read widely on the problems posed by some of the cases.

Essay question advice

Essays usually ask you about:

- The status of licences – you may have to link the material here with that on leases in Chapter 7.
- The extent to which a licence can confer a proprietary right.
- The nature of estoppel.

None of these is unduly technical, but you do need to learn the cases well!

Note also that you may be asked about how estoppel can be used to create other rights and the material has been designed with this type of question in mind as well.

Problem question advice

Problem questions are most likely to be on an estoppel situation and here you need to be absolutely clear on the requirements for estoppel to apply and be able to use the cases well. It may well be linked to the question of whether the estoppel right binds third parties. The other possibility is a question on whether a licence binds a third party and here it is essential that you are clear what is the present law and what *was* the law!

Sample questions

Could you answer these questions? Have a look at the questions which follow. They are examples of a typical essay question and a typical problem question. This chapter will cover the issues raised in these questions and review the law necessary to provide a comprehensive answer. Guidelines on answering the problem question will be provided at the end of the chapter and guidelines on answering the essay question are on the companion website for this book.

ESSAY QUESTION

'To what extent can a licence be considered to create a proprietary interest in land?' Consider this question by reference to decided cases.

PROBLEM QUESTION

Emily was the daughter of Claire, who has recently died. When Claire was aged 50, Emily gave up her job as a solicitor to move in and look after her mother, and she continued to do this until Claire died recently aged 82. Claire had been disabled and there was an informal arrangement that Claire's incapacity benefit would be paid to Emily to meet the needs of them both. In addition, Emily drew a carer's allowance for looking after her mother. Utility and other bills were paid out of Claire's savings.

Claire said to Emily on many occasions: 'I don't know what I would do without you. When I am gone you will have a secure home.' Emily assumed that Claire meant that she would leave her the house.

Claire has died intestate and has left seven children, including Emily, and under the intestacy rules the house will go to them equally.

Advise Emily on whether she has any rights in the house which are binding on the other children.

Would your answer differ if all the other children had signed a document ten years ago stating that, when Claire died, they would allow Emily to remain at the house?

■ What are licences?

A **licence** is permission from an owner of land (licensor) to the licensee to use the land for a specific purpose.

In general, licences are different from all the other rights in this book, as they are not property rights. The classic definition comes from this case:

KEY CASE

Thomas v. *Sorrell* (1673) Vaugh 330

Concerning: nature of licences

Legal principle

'A licence properly passeth no interest nor alters or transfers property in any thing, but only makes an action lawful which without it had been unlawful.'

There are various types of licences:

Bare licences

Bare licences are licences given without any consideration from the licensee, i.e. when you are invited to someone's house for a party.

Licences coupled with a grant

A **licence coupled with a grant** is where the licence is linked to an interest in the land, e.g. a licence to go on to land to collect wood. The right to collect wood is a profit.

It is misleading to talk at all of licences here, as the right to go on to the land is really part of the profit. These licences will last as long as the right to which they are attached.

Contractual licences

KEY DEFINITION

A **contractual licence** is where a licence is given for consideration.

Problem area

At common law, contractual licences and bare licences can, in principle, be revoked, at any time, although equitable remedies may be used to restrain a breach. There is no problem with bare licences but where a person has paid for a licence it has seemed unfair for it be capable of being revoked and this has led to a good deal of case law.

Example

I pay £100 for a ticket to a Test Match and travel a long way to the ground. I go in to the ground and am just starting to enjoy the game when an attendant tells me to leave. I ask the reason but I am just told to go and, when I refuse, I am forcibly ejected. It turns out that I had been mistaken for someone else who was a troublemaker.

EXAM TIP

The topic of revocability of licences is a favourite one in essays and you should read the different cases carefully. Make sure that you stress this one simple point: should a licence be able to be revoked (cancelled) at any time or should it be treated as an interest in land, like other land law rights?

REVISION NOTES

Licences are also important in connection with leases because a licencee of property has no security. Check Chapter 7 to make sure that you understand this. You could bring this point into your essay on licences.

Wood v. *Leadbitter* (1845) 13 M&W 838

Concerning: nature of licences

Facts

The claimant bought a ticket (which gave him a licence) for the Doncaster races but was ordered to leave. He refused and was physically ejected and claimed for assault.

Legal principle

A licence does not grant an interest in land and so may be revoked.

When equitable remedies became available in all courts after the Judicature Acts 1873–5 the position of licencees improved as equitable remedies were available, in particular, injunctions.

Hurst v. *Picture Theatres Ltd* [1915] 1 KB 1

Concerning: licence coupled with an interest in land

Facts

The claimant bought a cinema ticket but was later asked to leave as it was wrongly thought that he had not paid. He successfully claimed damages for assault.

Legal principle

He had a licence coupled with an interest in the land. The fact that he did not have a deed did not prevent this as equity will enforce written agreements under the principle in *Walsh* v. *Lonsdale* (1882).

REVISION NOTE

Check that you know and can apply the principle in *Walsh* v. *Lonsdale* (1882) – go to Chapter 7.

This decision was, and is, generally regarded as wrong, as there was no evidence that the claimant actually had an interest in the land. A right to watch a film does not give a proprietary right over the land.

Look at the judgment of Latham CJ in the Australian case of *Cowell* v. *Rosehill Racecourse Co. Ltd* (1937), where he pointed out that the decision in *Hurst* 'ignores the distinction between a personal and a property right'.

REVISION NOTE

Check that you are familiar with the idea of proprietary rights over the land as distinct from personal rights, which is all that the claimant seemed to have here – see Chapter 1.

KEY CASE

Winter Garden Theatre (London) Ltd v. *Millennium Productions Ltd* [1947] 2 All ER 331

Concerning: revocability of licences

Facts

A licence was granted to the respondents to present plays in a theatre. The court held that it could be revoked on giving reasonable notice.

Legal principle

Although this remedy was not granted in this case, the House of Lords held that revocation of a licence could be prevented where possible by an injunction. However, this does not make a licence an interest in land.

This case shows the possibility of the use of one equitable remedy to restrain breach of a licence. This next case shows another.

KEY CASE

Verrall v. *Great Yarmouth Borough Council* [1980] 1 All ER 839

Concerning: use of the equitable remedy of specific performance (SP) to restrain breach of an injunction

Facts

The council granted a contractual licence to the National Front to hold its annual conference on the pier at Yarmouth. This was later revoked.

Legal principle

SP would be granted to enforce the licence.

Contractual licences and third parties

As we saw above, the courts do not regard a licence as creating an interest in land, although they will use equitable remedies to restrain revocation of a licence in breach of contract. Logically, this should mean that a licence should never bind third parties but the courts have often attempted to make licences bind them.

EXAM TIP

This is a favourite topic for essay questions.

A good starting point is this case, which lays down the orthodox view:

KEY CASE

***King* v. *David Allen & Sons, Billposting Ltd* [1916] AC 54**

Concerning: is a contractual licence binding on third parties?

Facts

A licence was granted allowing the fixing of advertisements to the wall of a cinema. The licensor then granted a lease of the cinema to a third party.

Principle

The grant of the lease had ended the contractual licence.

EXAM TIP

This is a good clear case to begin an essay on this topic.

The history of attempts to make contractual licences binding on third parties can begin with this case:

Errington v. *Errington and Woods* **[1952] 1 All ER 149**

Concerning: are contractual licences binding on third parties?

Facts

An agreement was made between a father and his son and daughter-in-law that if they would pay the mortgage instalments due on a house he would convey the house to them. The father then died and the licence was held to bind the father's widow.

Legal principle

A contractual licence can bind third parties.

FURTHER THINKING

The above case makes a good departure point for some lateral thinking which could earn you extra marks. There could have been four other outcomes:

- The contract between the father on the one hand and the son and daughter-in-law on the other could have been binding on the widow as an estate contract as she was not a purchaser. (Title to the land was unregistered.)
- Did the widow sue in the capacity of personal representative of her husband's estate? The court did not consider this but if it had it could have held that she was bound.
- Did the son and daughter-in-law have a claim based on estoppel as they had paid the mortgage instalments acting on the father's representation that he would transfer the house to them?
- Could it have been argued that a constructive trust arose in their favour?

REVISION NOTES

Check:

- Chapter 2 for unregistered land.
- This chapter for estoppel.
- This chapter and Chapter 5 for constructive trusts.

Following this decision, the next significant development was the attempt to link the licence to a constructive trust to make it bind third parties.

Binions v. Evans [1972] 2 All ER 70

Concerning: use of a constructive trust to make a licence into a proprietary interest

Facts

Following her husband's death, the defendant was allowed by his employers to live rent free in the cottage which they had occupied. The employers then sold it to the claimants subject to their agreement with the defendant.

Legal principle

They took the property subject to a constructive trust in favour of the defendant.

Problem area

This case is controversial in the law of trusts for the way in which the constructive trust was used. However, it is a good example of how a licence can, in some circumstances, be elevated into a proprietary right by being held on a constructive trust.

FURTHER THINKING

Why did the court not simply hold that the defendant had a lease? The reasons were:

▌ There was no maximum duration.
▌ If it was argued that it was a lease for life, then s.149(6) LPA 1925 requires that rent must be payable.

REVISION NOTE

Check Chapter 7 for the requirements for a valid lease.

Both *Errington* v. *Errington* (1952) and *Binions* v. *Evans* (1972) were examples of a long attempt by Lord Denning to confer the status of a proprietary interest on contractual licences. The next case now represents the law and it shows that, whilst the decision in *Binions* v. *Evans* is good law, the idea that a contractual licence can be a proprietary interest in land is dead. The result is that *Errington* v. *Errington* is no longer good law.

Use *Errington* v. *Errington* in essay questions but not in problem questions as an answer to what the law is today.

Ashburn Anstalt v. *Arnold* [1988] 2 All ER 147

Concerning: are contractual licences binding on third parties?

Facts

The defendant sold its sublease but was allowed to remain in occupation of the premises until required to leave by the purchaser. The clamant bought the freehold expressly subject to this agreement. The actual decision was that the defendant was a lessee and so the claimant was bound, but the court considered what the result would have been had they had a licence.

Legal principle

A contractual licence does not give an interest in land. However, the court may impose a constructive trust where it is satisfied that the conscience of the existing owner is affected but it is not sufficient just that the land was sold subject to an agreement as in this case. The decision in *Binions* v. *Evans* was considered on its facts to be a good example of the circumstances when a constructive trust might be imposed.

Read Sparkes (1988) 104 LQR 175 for a commentary on this important decision. You should also look at other cases such as *DHN Food Distributors* v. *Tower Hamlets LBC* (1976) and *Lyus* v. *Prowsa Developments Ltd* (1982).

Estoppel licences

Estoppel arises where one person (the representee) has been led to act on the representation of another (the representor). If so, and if the representee then acts to their detriment on the basis of this promise, then in equity the court may grant them a remedy.

Estoppel licences can be used to grant rights other than licences and it is important to note that some of the cases discussed in connection with estoppel licences have in fact resulted in another right. You may get a question in the exam on estoppel in general and you should be prepared for this.

EXAM TIP

Note that estoppel is an example of equity: this means that there is a good deal of discretion in this area and it is unwise to come to a black and white conclusion.

Example

X owns a piece of land and says to Y: 'You can have it as a market garden.' Y takes over the land and develops it as a market garden but the land is never conveyed to him. X later attempts to turn Y out.

Here there is no conveyance, but equity feels that it could be unjust to allow a person in X's position to rely on this fact and so this injustice may be remedied by the doctrine of proprietary estoppel.

REVISION NOTE

You can see from the above example another instance of equity intervening where formalities have not been complied with. Check Chapter 1 to make sure that you remember another instance of this – equity enforcing agreements where there is no deed.

The essential elements of estoppel are:

■ an assurance by one person to another;
■ which is relied by that other person;
■ this reliance is to their detriment;
■ it would be unconscionable for the party making the assurance to go back on it.

KEY CASE

Inwards v. *Baker* **[1965] 1 All ER 446**

Concerning: licence created by estoppel

Facts
A father allowed his son to build a bungalow on land owned by the father.

Legal principle
The son was granted a licence for life.

The next case does not illustrate licences but it does show the principles of estoppel in action.

KEY CASE

Gilllett v. *Holt* [2000] 2 All ER 289

Concerning: estoppel

Facts

Holt promised Gillett on several occasions that he would leave him his farm in his will and, on the basis of this, Gillett worked as Holt's farm manager at a lower wage than he could have received elsewhere.

Legal principle

Holt was estopped from going back on his promise. As he had now made a will leaving the farm to another (X), the court directed that on Holt's death the farm was to be held on trust by X for Gillett.

Consequences of estoppel

▌ The court has a discretion as to the remedy – compare the two cases above.
▌ A right by estoppel may bind a purchaser where title to the land is registered.

KEY STATUTORY PROVISION

Section 116 of the Land Registration Act 2002

This allows an equity by estoppel to be registered and can take effect from the moment it arises. Therefore, it can be protected by a notice against the title.

In addition, if the person claiming the estoppel is in occupation under it, they may have an overriding interest under Sch.3, para. 2 LRA 2002.

REVISION NOTE

Check your knowledge of registered land principles by looking through Chapter 2.

Chapter summary
Putting it all together

☐ Can you tick all the points from the **revision checklist** at the beginning of this chapter?

☐ Take the **end-of-chapter quiz** on the companion website.

☐ Test your knowledge of the **key cases** with the **revision flashcards** on the website.

☐ Recall the legal principles of the **key cases** and **key statutory provisions** in this chapter.

☐ Attempt the **problem question** which was set out at the beginning of this chapter. See below for a final guide to it.

☐ Go to the companion website to test yourself on the **essay question** at the start of this chapter, and try out other questions.

Answer guidelines

See problem question at the start of the chapter.

Visual guide

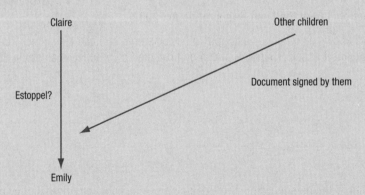

Claire

Other children

Estoppel?

Document signed by them

Emily

Apply conditions for an estoppel:
Representation – informal arrangement – what Claire said?
Relied on by Emily? Emily assumed that Claire meant that Emily would leave her the house.
To Emily's detriment? Note that Emily drew a carer's allowance.
Unconscionability?

If Emily succeeds then:

What will the remedy be? Court has a discretion.
Document signed by the children – does it mean that Emily's rights bind them? Look at e.g. *Binions* v. *Evans* (1972), *Ashburn Anstalt* v. *Arnold* (1988).
Her right could be registered (S.116 LRA 2002).

Making your answer stand out
Remember to discuss the land registration angle and demonstrate your ability to discuss cases such as *Ashburn Anstalt* in detail.

9
Easements and profits

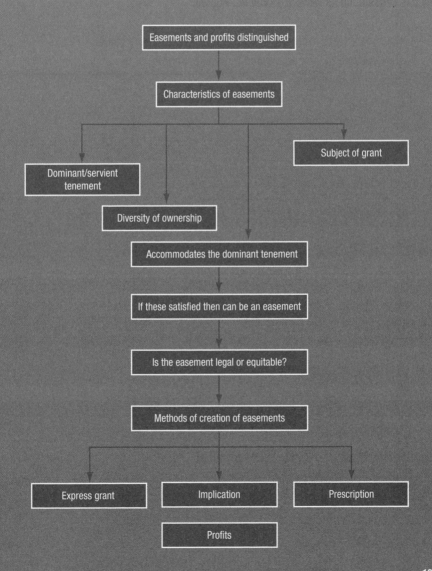

Easements and profits distinguished

Characteristics of easements

Dominant/servient tenement

Subject of grant

Diversity of ownership

Accommodates the dominant tenement

If these satisfied then can be an easement

Is the easement legal or equitable?

Methods of creation of easements

Express grant

Implication

Prescription

Profits

Revision checklist

What you need to know

- [ ] What is an easement?
- [ ] What is a profit?
- [ ] Characteristics of easements
- [ ] When an easement is a legal interest
- [ ] When an easement is an equitable interest
- [ ] How easements can be created by express grant/reservation
- [ ] How easements can be created by implication
- [ ] Three methods of prescription
- [ ] Characteristics of profits
- [ ] How rules on profits differ from easements

Introduction
Understanding easements and profits

Questions are usually on easements, but watch for one on a profit. They can easily slip in, such as one on grazing rights. You should watch for a possible connection with licences (Chapter 8). Another link is with land registration – check Chapters 2 and 3. The basic principles are fairly straightforward, but do watch for tricky areas such as the application of the rule in *Wheeldon* v. *Burrows* (1879) and the grant of easements under s.62(1) of the LPA 1925.

Essay question advice

This is a good subject for essays. Possible topics include:

- Can new negative easements be created?
- The rules on the grant of implied easements.
- Possible reform of the law on acquisition of easements by prescription.

Problem questions usually follow a familiar pattern, which requires you to deal with the following areas. You must address all of these issues:

- Can the right be an easement or a profit at all? At this stage you may eliminate some of the rights which may only be licences.
- If it is, is it legal or equitable? This will involve you in considering the third point:
- Was it correctly created?

Sample questions

Could you answer these questions? Have a look at the questions which follow. They are examples of a typical essay question and a typical problem question. This chapter will cover the issues raised in these questions and review the law necessary to provide a comprehensive answer. Guidelines on answering the problem question will be provided at the end of the chapter and guidelines on answering the essay question are on the companion website for this book.

Essay question

Many easements are implied rather than created by express grant. Critically analyse the methods by which easements can be created by implication.

Problem question

Freda owned 'The Retreat', a freehold property with registered title. This consists of a cottage with some land which has a small pond on it. She sold the cottage to Frank, who asks your advice on the following points:

(a) Freda agreed with Martin that Martin could have a right of access across her land in order to reach the pond and fish from it. The agreement was in writing and signed by both parties.
(b) Freda had orally agreed with a neighbour, Alfred, that Alfred could store firewood on part of her land and she then granted a lease of this part of the land to him.

■Easements and profits distinguished

Similarities: both easements and profits (in full, 'profits à prendre') are proprietary interests in land.
Difference: easements are rights over the land of another, e.g. rights to light, rights of way.

Profits are rights to enter on the land of another and take the profits of it e.g. fish, peat, wood.

This chapter first deals with easements and looks at profits at the end. This is because you are more likely to get exam questions on easements.

Characteristics of easements

In *Re Ellenborough Park* (1955) it was held that an easement must have four characteristics:

- Dominant/servient tenement.
- Diversity of ownership.
- Accommodates the dominant tenement.
- Subject of grant.

Dominant/servient tenement

This means that an easement must benefit land and there must be two pieces of land:

Example

Dominant tenement

Servient tenement

Owner of this has a right of way over ⟶ This.

Diversity of ownership

The dominant tenement (DT) and the servient tenement (ST) must be owned or occupied by different persons.

Accommodates the dominant tenement

This is a difficult term. It really means that the easement must benefit the land (DT) as such and not the present owner nor activities which the present owner is carrying on.

KEY CASE

Hill v. *Tupper* [1863] 2 H & C 121

Concerning: easement must accommodate (benefit) the DT

Facts

The owner of a canal granted X the exclusive right to put pleasure boats on the canal for profit.

Legal principle

Such a right is just a personal right which did not benefit the land as such.

The question is whether a business carried on on the land is so closely connected with the land that it does benefit it. This seems to be the explanation of the next case.

KEY CASE

Moody v. *Steggles* (1879) 12 Ch D 261

Concerning: whether a sign advertising a business could be an easement

Facts

It was held that a sign advertising a public house which was on neighbouring land was an easement.

Legal principle

Where the business is so closely connected with the land (i.e. the public house was in effect identified with the land on which it stood) then a sign advertising it can be an easement.

It follows that the DT and the ST must be reasonably adjacent otherwise there could be no benefit.

Example

X claims a right of way over land owned by Y but Y's land is two miles away. Although it may benefit X to have the right of way, it can hardly be said to benefit X's land.

Subject of a grant

The right claimed must be capable of forming the subject matter of a grant. The basic point is that the right must be sufficiently certain.

Example

X claims that Y should not build on his land as it would spoil X's view.

A right to a view is not certain enough to be an easement (*Aldred's Case* (1610)).

REVISION NOTE

X should have obtained a restrictive covenant over Y's land. Check Chapter 10.

This principle also means that:

■ Easements should not involve the owner of the ST in positive obligations

KEY CASE

Regis Property v. *Redman* [1956] 2 All ER 335

Concerning: positive easements

Facts

Claim to an easement of hot water and central heating.

Legal principle

This could not be an easement as it involved the owner of the ST in positive obligations.

FURTHER THINKING

There are cases where positive easements have been allowed – the obvious example is an easement of fencing.

Other points on easements:

■ No new negative easements?

KEY CASE

Phipps v. *Pears* [1964] 2 All ER 35

Concerning: creation of new negative easements (i.e. owner of ST has no actual obligations but is restricted in the use of the land)

Facts
Claim to an easement to protection of one house from rain and frost by another house. This would mean that the other house could not be demolished. The claim was rejected.

Legal principle
The courts are reluctant to allow the creation of new negative easements which would be an undue restriction on an owner's rights over his land.

FURTHER THINKING

This case was distinguished in *Rees* v. *Skerrett* (2001).You may get an essay question on the extent to which the courts are prepared to extend the categories of easements.

▍ Easement cannot amount to exclusive use.

KEY CASE

Copeland v. *Greenhalf* [1952] 1 All ER 809

Concerning: claim to an easement where there is exclusive use

Facts
The claimant owned land on which the defendant had stored and repaired vehicles for 50 years. He claimed an easement by prescription.

Legal principle
This was in effect a claim to beneficial use of the land and so could not be an easement.

FURTHER THINKING

Creation of easements by statute: example: Access to Neighbouring Land Act 1992. This Act can arise in an exam question so do check it!

■ Easements, profits and third parties

REVISION NOTE

The rules were set out in Chapters 2 and 3 and you should refer to these now to check your knowledge.

Summary

Registered land:

■ New legal easements and profits created expressly (i.e. by deed) are registrable dispositions.

■ Existing express legal easements and profits remain overriding.

■ Equitable easements and profits can now be protected registered interests (minor interests).

■ The only new legal easements and profits that can be overriding are those:
  - created by implied grant (rule in *Wheeldon* v. *Burrows* (1879) or s.62(1) LPA 1925);
  - created by prescription (Sch.3, para.3 LRA 2002).

Unregistered land:

■ Legal easements are binding on all third parties.

■ Equitable easements must be registered as Class D (iii) land charges if created on or after 1 January 1926. Those created before this date will bind purchasers who have notice of them and will bind donees automatically.

Express grant

■ Legal – deed.
■ Equitable – written agreement.

REVISION NOTE

You should check Chapter 1 and revise the rules on creation of legal interests in land by deed and equitable interests by written agreement.

Implication

■ Necessity, e.g. to land-locked land.
■ Estoppel.

Check Chapter 8 for estoppel. A good case on estoppel easements for the exam is *ER Ives Investments Ltd* v. *High* (1967).

▌ Acquisition of implied easements under the rule in *Wheeldon* v. *Burrows*.

KEY CASE

Wheeldon v. *Burrows* (1879) 12 Ch D 31

Concerning: acquisition of an easement by implied grant

Legal principle

On a grant of land, the grantee (e.g. the buyer) will acquire, by implication, all easements which:

▌ are continuous and apparent;
▌ have been and are at the time of the grant used by the grantor for the benefit of the land.

Note: the Legal principle above was strictly *obiter* and the facts would not add to your understanding.

You can recognise a *Wheeldon* v. *Burrows* situation because there will be a plot of land which is originally in the ownership of one person and is then subdivided.

Wheeldon v. *Burrows* easements operate in favour of the buyer and against the seller.

This is how a *Wheeldon* v. *Burrows* situation works:

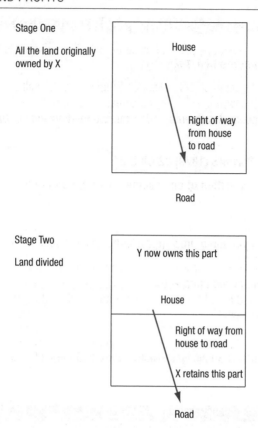

Rule in *Wheeldon* v. *Burrows*: this allows Y to claim as an implied easement of a right of way over the land retained by X.

Note that the rule in *Wheeldon* v. *Burrows* also applies where X in the above example sells all the land and grants part of the land to one person (Y) in our example, and grants the other part to Z (i.e. the part retained by X in our example). Therefore, X no longer retains any land.

Are easements created by the rule in *Wheeldon* v. *Burrows* legal or equitable? This depends on the document which transferred the land (e.g. the document under which X transferred land to Y).

If it was a deed (which it would be here), then the easement will be legal, but if was simply by an enforceable written contract it will be equitable.

REVISION NOTE

Go back to Chapter 1 and check that you understand the distinction between deeds and written agreements.

■ Acquisition of implied easements under s.62(1) LPA 1925.

KEY STATUTORY PROVISION

Section 62(1) of the LPA 1925

'A conveyance of land shall be deemed to include and shall ... operate to convey, with the land, all ... privileges, easements, rights ... appertaining or reputed to appertain to the land ... at the time of conveyance ...'

KEY CASE

Wright v. *Macadam* [1949] 2 All ER 565

Concerning: operation of s.62(1) LPA 1925 so that it creates new easements in addition to transferring existing easements

Facts

The defendant let a flat to the claimant and gave her permission (i.e. a licence) to store coal in it. He later granted her a new tenancy.

Legal principle

The grant of the tenancy was a conveyance under s.62(1) LPA 1925 and, as a right to store coal was a right capable of being granted by law, the grant of the new tenancy had the effect of converting what was a tenancy into an easement.

Permission to store coal (Licence)   New lease   Permission now an easement

EXAM TIP

Always check that the right is capable of being an easement. In fact in *Wright* v. *Macadam* the right of storage appeared to be exclusive, which ought not to have qualified it for an easement. In a problem question the answer would be that exclusive right of storage was *not* an easement.

There has been much debate on whether 'diversity of occupation' is needed for the principle in *Wright* v. *Macadam* to apply, i.e. is it necessary for each piece of land to be occupied by different people? Look at *Sovmots Investments Ltd* v. *Secretary of State for the Environment* (1977) and especially the speech in the House of Lords of Lord Wilberforce.

■Prescription

This is not likely to be the subject of a whole exam question but it can form part of it.

KEY DEFINITION

Prescription means acquisition of easements and profits by long use.

Conditions for prescription:
Use must be without:

■ Force.
■ Secrecy.
■ Permission.

Types of prescription

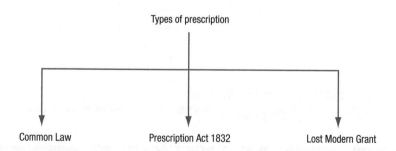

Types of prescription

Common Law   Prescription Act 1832   Lost Modern Grant

■ Common law – from 'time immemorial' – 1189 – in practice for as long as anyone can remember and it could have been since 1189.

If the DT is a house then this method cannot apply as the house will not have existed in 1189.

■ Under the Prescription Act 1832.

KEY STATUTORY PROVISION

Section 2 of the Prescription Act 1832

Claim to an easement by prescription requires 20 years' continuous use, but where the easement was exercised with the oral agreement of the owner of the ST it is 40 years.

Note: periods for profits: 30 and 60 years.

KEY STATUTORY PROVISION

Section 3 of the Prescription Act 1832

Claim to an easement of light requires 20 years' continuous use – no provision for an extra 20 years where exercised with the permission of the owner.

Note: Rights of Light Act 1959: owner of ST can block a right to light by registering a notice.

KEY STATUTORY PROVISION

Section 4 of the Prescription Act 1832

The periods must be 'next before' the action.

Discontinuance for less than a year ignored.
The relationship between these sections is shown by this example:

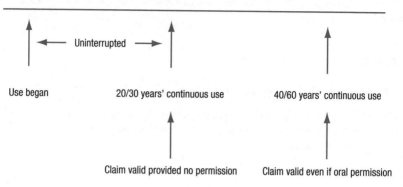

■ Lost modern grant

In an exam question this should be mentioned as the last possibility.

KEY DEFINITION

The doctrine of the lost modern grant states that if there has been 20 years' continuous use which is without force, secrecy or permission, then an easement was granted before the use began but the deed of grant has been lost.

The court assumes two things that have not in fact occurred:

■ There was a grant of an easement.
■ It has been lost.

Example

This is based on a profit.
X has allowed his sheep to graze on Y's land for many years but did not do so for the last 18 months because they were diseased.

■ No claim to a profit at common law: cannot prove use since 1189.
■ Prescription Act does not apply as discontinuance more than a year – s.4 applies – no period of prescription as period not next before action.
■ So have to rely on lost modern grant.

See *Tehidy Minerals Ltd* v. *Norman* (1971) for a case example.

▌Profits

Check carefully what the right is: an easement or a profit.

Note the following rules on profits and how they differ from those on easements:

▐ No requirement of a dominant tenement.
▐ The rule in *Wheeldon* v. *Burrows* (1879) does not apply to the creation of profits but s.62(1) LPA 1925 does.
▐ The periods of prescription are longer (see above).
▐ Apart from this, the rules are generally the same.

Chapter summary
Putting it all together

Answer guidelines

See the problem question at the start of the chapter.

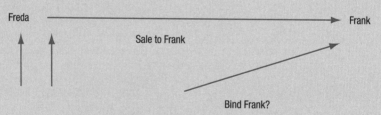

Rights granted to: Martin, Freda

Martin: Right of access to pond to fish in it = profit. Equitable – no deed. Was it protected on the register? If not, not binding on Frank.

Alfred: Oral agreement – is it an easement – right of exclusive storage? If it can be an easement then although the actual agreement is equitable it may be converted into a legal easement by s.62(1) LPA 1925: *Wright* v. *McAdam* (1949). If so, can be overriding: apply Sch.3, para. 3 LRA 2002.

Making your answer stand out
Make sure that you look carefully at the question of whether Alfred's easement could be overriding under the LRA 2002. Many students miss this point.

10
Covenants affecting freehold land

```
┌─────────────────────────────┐
│  Covenants on freehold land │
│   (restrictive covenants)   │
└─────────────────────────────┘
              │
              ▼
┌─────────────────────────────┐
│   Terminology and positive  │
│   and negative covenants    │
└─────────────────────────────┘
              │
              ▼
┌─────────────────────────────┐     ┌─────────────────────────┐
│ Liability of the original   │     │  Rights of non-parties  │
│ parties – the covenantor    │     │      (Situation 2)      │
│ and the covenantee          │     └─────────────────────────┘
│      (Situation 1)          │
└─────────────────────────────┘
       │                 │
       ▼                 ▼
┌──────────────────────┐  ┌──────────────────────────────┐
│       Burden         │  │          Benefit             │
│ Liability on the     │  │ Enforcement of the covenant: │
│ covenant; the        │  │ the covenantee and           │
│ covenantor and       │  │ successors in title          │
│ successors in title  │  │      (Situation 4)           │
│   (Situation 3)      │  │                              │
└──────────────────────┘  └──────────────────────────────┘
            Situation 5
          combines 3 and 4
              │
              ▼
┌─────────────────────────────┐
│        Discharge of         │
│    restrictive covenants    │
└─────────────────────────────┘
              │
              ▼
┌─────────────────────────────┐
│    Remedies for breach of   │
│    a restrictive covenant   │
└─────────────────────────────┘
```

Revision checklist

What you need to know:

- [ ] What a restrictive covenant is
- [ ] Distinction between positive and negative covenants
- [ ] The liability of the original covenantor
- [ ] When s.56(1) of the LPA 1925 could apply to a situation
- [ ] The common law rules on when the benefit of a restrictive covenant may run
- [ ] The equitable rules on when the benefit of a restrictive covenant may run
- [ ] The situations when the burden of a restrictive covenant may run at common law
- [ ] The rules on when the burden of a restrictive covenant may run in equity
- [ ] The remedies which may be given for breach of a restrictive covenant

Introduction
Understanding restrictive covenants

This is an area which students often avoid when revising for examinations. This is a shame, as the basic idea is simple: John owns a large area of land. He sells part of it (Blackacre) to Rosemary but keeps Whiteacre on which he had a house. As he is still going to live nearby, he wants to retain some control over the use that can be made of it. Therefore he imposes restrictions in the transfer to Rosemary which are known as **restrictive covenants**. There are other rules which are not complex in themselves: the problem is seeing how they relate to each other. Make sure that you can do this.

Essay question advice

This tends to be an area for problems rather than essays but a typical essay will ask you to discuss whether the present law needs reforming. To answer this you need:

- A thorough knowledge of problem areas in the current law, e.g. why are there different rules for positive and negative covenants and why are there different rules for the running of the benefit and burden in equity as distinct from the common law?
- Proposals for reform.

An alternative is a straightforward question asking you to outline the present rules.

Problem question advice

All examination problem questions in this area usually begin with the scenario mentioned in the introduction above and there are two fundamental questions:

▮ Who is bound by the restrictive covenant?
▮ Who can enforce it?

Keep these two questions in your mind throughout your answer. Once you have mastered this scenario the good news is that virtually all restrictive covenants questions follow this pattern – there are unlikely to be many variations.

Remember this checklist:

▮ Who is the covenantor and who is the covenantee?
▮ Which covenants are positive and which are negative?
▮ Is title to the land registered or unregistered?

Sample questions

Essay question

'The rules on whether covenants or freehold land can give rights and impose obligation on subsequent owners are absurdly complex and in need of reform.' Discuss.

Problem question

John owns a large area of land. He sells part of it (Blackacre) to Rosemary but keeps Whiteacre on which he had a house. As he is still going to live nearby, he wants to retain some control over the use that can be made of Blackacre. Therefore, he imposes restrictions in the transfer to Rosemary which are known as **restrictive covenants.** These are:

(a) That no business shall be carried on on Blackacre.
(b) That all fences must be kept in repair.
(c) That the owner of Blackacre shall contribute to the maintenance of the sewers which serve both Blackacre and Whiteacre.

These covenants are expressed to be for the benefit of Blackacre.

Rosemary subsequently sells Blackacre to Aidan and John sells Whiteacre to Eileen. Aidan has decided to run his accountancy business from Blackacre and is seeking planning permission from the local authority to enable him to do this. He has failed to repair the fences and he refuses to contribute to the maintenance of the sewers.

Advise Eileen on any action which she may take against Aidan to enforce the covenants. Title to both Blackacre and Whiteacre is registered.

Note: These covenants will be used as examples throughout this chapter and will be referred to as the standard covenants.

■ Covenants on freehold land

Before we go into more detail, make sure you revise and remember the following terms.

■ *Covenants on freehold land*: Some examples of restrictive covenants were given in the question above. 'Covenants' are simply promises contained in deeds and, as a transfer of the freehold title to land must be by deed (s.52(1) LPA 1925), Rosemary's promises to John in the above scenario are called covenants.

■ *Restrictive covenants*: A restrictive covenant is simply a type of covenant which restricts the use of land (e.g. it provides that the land shall not be built on). The word 'restrictive' in this topic is in fact misleading, although the term will be used in this chapter as it is so commonly used.

■ *Positive and negative covenants*: Covenants on land are of two types: positive and negative.

EXAM TIP

Knowing the distinction between positive and negative covenants is vital to answering a question on this area. Indeed, if you are unsure of the distinction, you should not even attempt to answer the question!

KEY DEFINITION

A **negative covenant** is a restrictive covenant which restricts the use to which the land may be put. The simplest test for distinguishing between positive and negative covenants is to ask if performance of them requires expenditure of money. If it does the covenant is positive.

■ *Covenants which 'touch and concern the land' and personal covenants*: The former phrase has been met before in Chapter 7 on leases and it means that the covenant must benefit the land itself. The real point is that the covenant must not be personal. An example of a personal covenant would be 'to do X's shopping for him'. Again, the importance of this distinction will become clear in Situation 3 below.

■ *The parties involved*: The person who agrees to the covenant is the **covenantor** and the person with whom the agreement is made with is the **covenantee**. In practice, the covenantor will be usually be the buyer of the land because the seller will have required the buyer to agree to the covenants as a condition of the sale. In the above question, Rosemary is the covenantor and John is the covenantee.

Your first step in answering a problem question on covenants should always be to identify the covenantor and covenantee.

■ *Benefit and burden*: Land to which the covenant applies is **burdened** by the covenant and so this will be land owned by the **covenantor**. Land owned by the **covenantee** is **benefited** by the covenant. Thus in the above question, Blackacre, owned by Rosemary, is the burdened land and Whiteacre, owned by John, is the benefited land.

■ *Registered and unregistered land*: Check the question carefully to see whether it states that the title to the burdened land is registered or unregistered. The significance of this will appear later but make a habit of putting this on your checklist.

REVISION NOTE

Go back to Chapters 2 and 3 and check that you know how restrictive covenants fit into the scheme of unregistered and unregistered land.

John is the original covenantee and Rosemary is the original covenantor.
Can John bring an action against Rosemary?

Warning!

Note that this chapter deals only with covenants on **freehold** land: leasehold covenants are dealt with in Chapter 7.

Although where the landlord wishes to sue a sub-tenant (not the tenant), the rules on restrictive covenants apply (see Chapter 7), exam questions will be most unlikely to mix up freehold and leasehold covenants and so this point will almost certainly only arise in a question on leasehold covenants. In short, the message is not to worry about leasehold covenants for now!

There are five basic situations that occur with restrictive covenants and problems in an examination will revolve around these. In this chapter we will explore each of these five different scenarios:

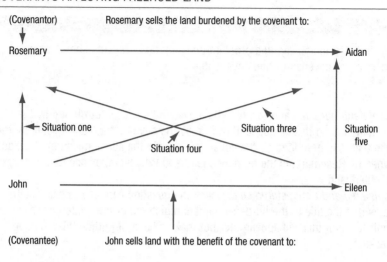

(Covenantor)   Rosemary sells the land burdened by the covenant to:

Rosemary ───► Aidan

Situation one   Situation three   Situation five

Situation four

John ───► Eileen

(Covenantee)   John sells land with the benefit of the covenant to:

Note: Situation Two is not shown here.

■ Situation One: liability of the original parties: the covenantor and the covenantee

John is the original covenantee and Rosemary is the original covenantor. Rosemary is in breach of the covenants.

Can John bring an action against Rosemary?

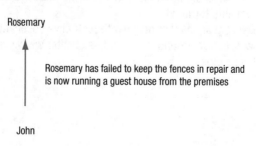

Rosemary

Rosemary has failed to keep the fences in repair and is now running a guest house from the premises

John

(a) The original parties can claim against each other on the covenant. In reality this means that John (the covenantor) can claim against (Rosemary) (the covenantee).

In the above situation, John can sue Rosemary on the standard covenants. As between the original parties all covenants are binding, which means that this basic rule applies to all covenants.

As will be seen later, when the rights of subsequent parties are involved the law distinguishes between these different types of covenants.

(b) The original covenantor may continue to be liable on the covenant even though he/she is no longer owner of the land. This rule is not only one of common law but is also implied by:

KEY STATUTORY PROVISION

Section 79(1) of the LPA 1925

'A covenant relating to any land of the covenantor . . . shall . . . be deemed to be made by the covenantor on behalf of himself and his successors in title.'

This means that the covenant can not only be binding on successors in title but that the original covenantor is liable for any breaches by successors in title. However, the rule in s.79(1) will not apply if the covenant provides that the liability of the original covenantor is to cease when he/she sells the land.

The effect of this is that if Rosemary sells Blackacre to Aidan, she needs to take a covenant from Aidan that he will comply with the standard covenants. Then if Aidan does breach them and Rosemary is sued by John, she can sue Aidan. When Aidan sells he should take a similar covenant from his buyer and so liability moves down the line with a chain of covenants, known as **indemnity covenants**.

■ Situation Two: rights of non-parties

This is the same scenario as Situation One but with an addition:

Rosemary enters into the standard covenants with John but also enters into the same covenants with 'the owners of land adjacent to the land conveyed'. This means that she has covenanted with the owners of land (Greensleaves) adjacent to John's land (Whiteacre), in this case Albert.

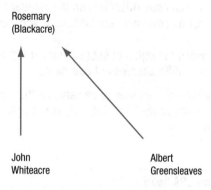

Rosemary
(Blackacre)

John
Whiteacre

Albert
Greensleaves

The right of Albert to enforce the covenant is contained in:

Section 56(1) of the LPA 1925

'A person may take ... the benefit of any condition, right of entry, covenant or agreement over or respecting land or other property, although he may not be named as a party to the conveyance or other instrument.'

KEY STATUTORY PROVISION

Thus, in our scenario – where the provision regarding adjacent landowners is spelled out in the covenant – s.56(1) would allow adjacent owners of land to sue. If there was no such clause in our scenario, then s.56(1) would not apply.

In any exam question, ask whether the person seeking to enforce the benefit of the covenant was in existence at the time the covenant was made. If the answer is yes, then she may be able to enforce the covenant subject to the test below.

KEY CASE

Re Ecclesiastical Commissioners for England's Conveyance [1936] Ch 430

Concerning: application of s.56(1) of the LPA 1925

Facts

The sellers had sold freehold plots adjacent to Blackacre and then, when Blackacre was sold, the purchaser of Blackacre entered into covenants with the sellers and also with those owners of adjacent land.

Legal principle

It was held that the adjacent landowners could enforce the covenants applying s.56(1) above.

Neuberger J in *Amsprop Trading Ltd* v. *Harris Distribution Ltd* (1997) quoted from *Megarry and Wade on The Law of Real Property* (5th edn 1984), which states: 'The true aim of section 56 seems to be not to allow a third party to sue on a contract merely because it is for his benefit; the contract must purport to be made with him', i.e. does the covenantor actually promise the covenantee that owners of adjacent land will benefit?

KEY STATUTORY PROVISION

Section 1 of the Contracts (Rights of Third Parties) Act 1999

A person who is not a party to a contract is able to take the benefit of a contractual term which purports to confer a benefit on him.

This Act covers the whole of the law of contract, not just this area, but in this area this Act and s.56(1) of the LPA 1925 overlap.

This wording clearly applies to our situation, as the covenant is contained in a contract and it confers a benefit on third parties, i.e. Albert as an adjoining landowner. Thus it can be seen that s.56(1) of the LPA and this Act overlap and a good answer would explain that either could be used.

It is possible to have wording which would allow Albert to claim under the Contracts (Rights of Third Parties) Act 1999 but not under s.56(1). Suppose that the wording was 'this covenant is entered into with the owners of all land adjoining Whiteacre', rather than the owners of land 'now or formerly forming part of Whiteacre'. In this case it could be argued that this could include Albert.

■Situation Three: liability on the covenant: the covenantor and successors in title

Before looking at the issues here it is vital to note one point: we are now going beyond the original parties and deciding whether subsequent parties to the covenant (i.e. successors in title) can sue to enforce them.

Common law and equity

The other point to note at this stage is that common law and equity have different rules and, broadly speaking, equity goes further than the common law in allowing the enforcement of covenants between successors in title of the original parties. The common law and equitable rules do not overlap and so the fact that they are mutually exclusive means that examination answers must carefully distinguish between them.

Situation Three in detail

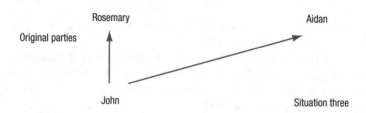

Original parties

Rosemary

John

Aidan

Situation three

Again, the starting position is Scenario One, with Rosemary and John as the original covenantor and covenantee. However, Rosemary now sells Blackacre to Aidan. John remains the owner of Whiteacre. Assume that Aidan is in breach of all the covenants. Can John bring an action against Aidan?

This section will consider in each case whether the **burden** of the covenant has passed to Aidan.

The answers are different in each case but initially we can leave standard covenant (c) until later and deal with (a) and (b).

Covenants (a) and (b)

The first thing that you should do with this situation is consider which of the covenants are positive and which are negative. The covenant in (a) is negative and in (b) is positive.

NOTE: the simplest test for distinguishing between positive and negative covenants is to ask whether performance of them requires expenditure of money.

The distinction between positive and negative covenants is vital because positive covenants generally only bind the original covenantor, i.e. Rosemary in the above question, and not subsequent parties, i.e. Aidan. Equity takes a different view and generally negative covenants can bind subsequent parties.

Before looking at the rules in more detail, keep the fundamental ones in mind:

▌ Positive covenants, with only a few exceptions, bind only the original parties.
▌ Negative covenants can bind subsequent parties in equity.

EXAM TIP

These rules will always appear in a problem question on covenants.

The rules on positive covenants in more detail

The common law rule on positive covenants was established in the following case.

KEY CASE
***Austerberry* v. *Oldham Corporation* (1885) 29 Ch D 750**
Concerning: positive covenants – not binding on subsequent owners of land
Legal principle
It was held that the burden of a covenant to keep a road in good repair could not bind a subsequent owner of the land.

The decision in *Austerberry* was followed in *Rhone* v. *Stephens* (1994). Applied to Situation Three, this means that the positive covenant (b) to keep all fences in repair *is not* binding on Aidan.

The rules on negative covenants in more detail

Equity takes a different view on negative covenants, as established in the following case:

Tulk v. *Moxhay* (1848) 2 Ph 774

Concerning: negative covenants – binding on subsequent owners of land

Legal principle

It was held that a covenant not to build on land in the middle of Leicester Square in London was binding on a subsequent purchaser of that land.

EXAM TIP

Never go into a Land Law exam without knowing this case!

Applied to our situation, and provided the conditions set out below are satisfied, the negative covenant (a) not to carry on a business *is* binding on Aidan.

Why did equity decide to enforce negative covenants? The decision in *Tulk* v. *Moxhay* was based on the fact that the purchaser had notice of the covenant.

REVISION NOTE

As you probably know by now, the term 'notice' has a particular meaning in Land Law, and if you are still uncertain what it means, refer back to Chapter 1 now to revise this.

Assuming that the covenant is negative, the following other conditions must be satisfied before equity will enforce it against subsequent parties:

1 **The covenantee must own land for the benefit of which the covenant was entered into.**

LCC v. *Allen* [1914] 3 KB 642

Concerning: negative covenants – covenantee must own the land for the benefit of which the covenant was entered into

Facts

A builder (X) was given permission by the LCC to lay out a new street on land and covenanted in return with the LCC, not to build on some land. The LCC did not own any land in the area at the time when the covenant was granted and so they could not enforce the covenant against building against a successor title of X.

Legal principle

The covenantee, in order to enforce the covenant against successors in title of the covenantor, must retain land which could be benefited by the covenant. In *Kelly* v. *Barrett* (1924) Pollock MR felt that a covenant restricting the use of land at Hampstead could be enforced by someone who owned land no nearer to Hampstead than Clapham (i.e. the other side of London).

2 **The covenant must touch and concern the dominant land.** As mentioned above, the point here is the covenant must not be personal.

REVISION NOTE

Check Chapter 7 (leases) to revise what this term means.

3 **It must be the common intention of the parties that the covenant shall run.** Covenants made on or after January 1926 are deemed to be made with subsequent parties (s.79 LPA 1925). Covenants made before that date will run if the language indicates this, e.g. 'the covenant is made by the covenantor for himself, his heirs and assigns'.

4 **The covenantee must have notice of the covenant.** It is a fundamental requirement of all equitable interests that they bind only persons with notice. (You should know this by now!) However, the notice requirement has been overridden by the increasing registration of title to land and the rules are now:

   (i) If title to the burdened land is registered, the covenant must be protected by a notice on the register of that title (s.29 LRA 2002). If it is not, the covenant will not bind a purchaser.

   (ii) If title to the land is not registered and the covenant was entered into on or after 1 January 1926 then it must be registered as a Class D(ii) land charge, otherwise it will not bind a purchaser.

(iii) If title to the land is not registered and the covenant was entered into before 1 January 1926 then the old notice rules apply and the covenant will not bind a purchaser unless he/she has notice of it (see Chapter 1 for a discussion of notice).

Note: If the covenant was not registered when Aidan bought Blackacre, then it would not bind him. However, it could be registered after he bought it and if Aidan sold Blackacre to Charles it would bind Charles.

Covenant (c)

This is a covenant by the owner of Blackacre to contribute to the maintenance of the sewers which serve *both* Blackacre and Whiteacre. As such it is a positive covenant and so it would not be enforceable against subsequent owners of Blackacre were it not for a special rule.

Covenants of this kind operate in situations where there are reciprocal benefits and burdens enjoyed by users of the facility. A mention of such a covenant in an examination question should lead you to mention the following:

KEY CASE

Halsall v. *Brizell* [1957] 1 All ER 371

Concerning: positive covenants – an exception when they are binding on subsequent owners

Facts

Buyers of building plots covenanted that they would contribute to the cost of repairs of sewers and roads that were for the common use of the owners of all the building plots.

Legal principle

It was held that an agreement to contribute to the cost of these repairs was binding on a subsequent owner on the principle that you cannot take the benefit of these rights yet not avoid the burdens of them.

FURTHER THINKING

Look at the judgment of Peter Gibson LJ in *Thamesmead Town Ltd.* v. *Allotey* (1998) for a detailed consideration of when the *Halsall* v. *Brizell* principle can apply.

When does this principle apply? The answer is not clear. In *Rhone* v. *Stephens* (1994) Lord Templeman said that it would not apply when the owner had no choice whether to accept both the benefit and the burden. It is probably on this basis that mutual covenants between neighbours to maintain a fence between their respective properties would not come under *Halsall* v. *Brizell*.

Finally, clarify whether this particular covenant is binding on Aidan.

∎ Situation Four: enforcing the benefit at common law: the covenantee and successors in title

John sells Whiteacre to Eileen, Rosemary remains the owner of Blackacre. Can Eileen bring an action against Rosemary? This involves the question of whether the **benefit** of the covenant has passed to Eileen.

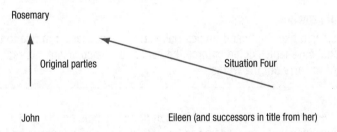

Rosemary

Original parties   Situation Four

John   Eileen (and successors in title from her)

We have already seen in Situation One that the covenantee (i.e. John) can enforce the standard covenants against the covenantor (i.e. Rosemary). We are now looking at whether successors in title to the covenantee can enforce the covenant, i.e. in our situation, whether Eileen can enforce the covenant. Remember that this will be enforcing the benefit of the covenant.

Note what was said in the introduction to Situation Three: common law and equity take different approaches and do not mix. The common law *will* allow Eileen, provided that certain conditions are met (see below), to enforce the covenants against Rosemary. This only applies to actions against **the original covenantor**.

Equitable rules will apply when we come to consider, in Situation Five, what happens when Rosemary sells Blackacre to Aidan.

The following conditions must be met for Eileen to be able to show that the benefit of the covenant has passed to her and that she can sue Rosemary for breach of them:

∎ The covenant **must touch and concern the land** (*Rogers* v. *Hosegood* (1900)). (See above under Situation Three for an explanation of this term.)

▌ The original covenantee must have had **a legal estate** in the land which is benefited.

▌ The successor in title (Eileen) must have also acquired a legal estate in the land.

▌ The benefit of the covenant was intended by the original parties to run with the land.

KEY CASE

Smith and Snipes Hall Farm v. *River Douglas Catchment Board* [1949] 2 All ER 179

Concerning: enforcing the benefit of covenants by a successor in title to the original covenantee

Facts

The Board (equivalent to Rosemary in our example) covenanted with Mrs Smith (who was in the position of John above) that they would carry out works to prevent her land from being flooded. Mrs Smith then sold the land to Smith and Snipes Hall Farm (equivalent to Eileen in our example).

Legal principle

It was held that Smith and Snipes Hall Farm as a successor in title to the original covenantee could enforce the benefit of the covenant, i.e. require the Board to carry out the works.

Note: A covenant not to allow pets other than domestic pets on the land is often found in exam questions and is considered to benefit the land (i.e. it touches and concerns the land).

▌Situation Five: enforcing the benefit in equity: successors in title to both covenantee and covenantor

John sells Whiteacre to Eileen, Rosemary sells Blackacre to Aidan. Aidan is in breach of all the standard covenants. Can Eileen bring an action against Aidan? This involves whether the **benefit** has passed to Eileen and the burden has **passed** to Aidan.

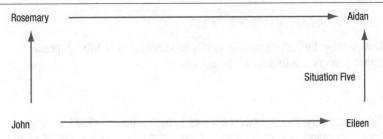

Note that the above rules in Situation Four are of no help at all where Eileen wishes to sue Aidan. If Eileen is to have a right to enforce against Aidan, then this can only be in equity because, as we saw in Situation Three, Aidan is only liable in equity.

There are three methods under which Eileen can show that the benefit of a covenant has passed to her **in equity**:

■ By annexation.
■ By assignment.
■ By proof of the existence of a building scheme.

Each of these will now be looked at in turn.

Annexation

The essence of annexation is that the benefit of the covenant is **attached to the land**; 'glued to it' may be a more vivid phrase. Whoever acquires title to the land benefited by the covenant (the dominant land) also acquires the benefit of the covenant.

This can happen in three ways:

■ **Express annexation.** Look at the words of the deed which created the covenant.

Rogers v. *Hosegood* [1900] 2 Ch 388

Concerning: benefit passed in equity to successors in title: express annexation of the benefit of the covenant

Facts

The deed stated that the covenant was to be for 'the benefit of the vendors, their successors and assigns and others claiming under them to all or any of their lands adjoining'.

Legal principle

Where the deed clearly shows an intention that the covenant shall be for the benefit of land which is identified in the covenant then the benefit of the covenant is expressly annexed to that land.

Contrast this case with *Renals* v. *Cowlishaw* (1878): covenant made with 'the covenantee, his heirs, executors and assigns' was not enough, as it did not identify which land was to be benefited.

EXAM TIP

Compare the wording of the covenant in an examination question with that in the above cases very carefully.

▌ **Implied annexation**. This is where there is no mention in the covenant that it benefits particular land and so any intention to annex the benefit of the covenant to the land must be implied.

Marten v. *Flight Refuelling Ltd* [1961] 2 All ER 696

Concerning: benefit passed in equity to successors in title: implied annexation

Facts

A covenant that the land would be used for agricultural purposes was made with the covenantee and 'its successors in title'.

Legal principle

This was held to be enough for the court to imply annexation, even though the covenant did not actually mention the land to be benefited.

▌ Statutory annexation.

KEY STATUTORY PROVISION

Section 78(1) of the LPA 1925

'A covenant relating to any land of the covenantee shall be deemed to be made with the covenantee and his successors in title.'

This includes all covenants which relate to the land but will not include personal covenants, e.g. 'to do X's shopping for her'.

KEY CASE

Federated Homes Ltd v. *Mill Lodge Properties Ltd* [1980] 1 All ER 371

Concerning: benefit passed in equity to successors in title: statutory annexation

Facts

In this case a covenant which prohibited the erection of more than 300 houses on land was enforceable by successors in title of the covenantee.

Legal principle

It was held that the effect of s.78 of the LPA 1925 was that any covenant relating to land must be read as if it was made with the covenantee and his successors in title, **even where there are no express words of annexation.**

FURTHER THINKING

Federated Homes has not escaped criticism. Look at, e.g., Newsome (1982) 98 LQR 202.

EXAM TIP

Federated Homes and *Tulk* v. *Moxhay* (1848) are the two absolutely vital cases to learn for the exam! The facts of *Federated Homes* are much less important than the decision.

The effect of the above case is that the benefit of a covenant will be annexed to land even where there are no words of the kind in *Rogers* v. *Hosegood* and so the cases where the benefit will not be annexed will be few. This means that most cases will now fall under the heading of statutory annexation although if the facts of an examination question are similar to those of *Rogers* v. *Hosegood* then it is as well to treat it as express annexation.

Problem areas

1 **Where the covenant cannot benefit the majority of the dominant land.** *Re Ballard's Conveyance* (1937): a covenant not to erect buildings other than dwelling houses on land could not benefit the whole of an estate of 1,700 acres. It will be a question of evidence in each case whether the covenant benefited all of the dominant land or not. (See also *Earl of Leicester* v. *Wells-next-the-Sea UDC* (1972)).
2 **Where the dominant land is later divided.**

Example

Suppose that Whiteacre was divided by Eileen and she retained part and part was sold to Josephine. Could they both claim the benefit of the covenant?

There is no clear answer here but it appears from *Federated Homes* that, unless the covenant clearly indicates that it is only to be annexed to the whole of the dominant land, the benefit will pass when the land is divided. Thus it is likely that Josephine can enforce it.

Assignment

This was once more significant than it is now and its importance was diminished by *Federated Homes*, which has made annexation the method of transferring the benefit of a covenant in the great majority of cases.

KEY CASE

Roake v. *Chadha* [1983] 3 All ER 503

Concerning: benefit passed in equity to successors in title: statutory annexation

Facts

A covenant stated that it could not endure for the benefit of successors in title unless this benefit was expressly assigned.

Legal principle

Thus, *Federated Homes* could not apply, as it was not possible to use the method of annexation because assignment was expressly required.

For higher marks, see also *Newton Abbot Co-operative Society* v. *Williamson and Treadgold* (1952); a useful case, as it deals with most of the requirements of assignment.

By proof of the existence of a building scheme

This is often found in practice.

Example

Suppose that in our situation John, instead of selling part of his land to Rosemary, decides to develop it all and to sell it in individual plots with houses on each plot. John wants the area to be kept tidy and to remain residential, as this will affect the price which he will be able to obtain for each plot. Therefore, he requires each buyer to enter into the following covenants with both the developers and with all other owners:

(a) not to run a business from their house;
(b) not to erect any fences, walls, hedges etc. in their front gardens.

The effect is to create a local law for that area and provided that the requirements for a building scheme are satisfied, then these covenants are enforceable.

KEY CASE

Elliston v. *Reacher* [1908] 2 Ch 374

Concerning: benefit passed in equity to successors in title: requirements for a building scheme

Legal principle

The requirements for a building scheme were set out as follows:

▌ Both parties derive their title from a common vendor.
▌ Prior to the sale to these parties, the developer laid out the estate in lots subject to restrictions intended to be imposed on all plots and which are consistent with a general scheme of development.
▌ The restrictions were intended to be imposed on all plots.
▌ Both claimant and defendant bought their land on the footing that the restrictions would be for the benefit of all the other plots included in the scheme of development.

EXAM TIP

This area can lend itself to essay questions in the exam. A careful look at the cases is recommended.

These requirements have been relaxed in more recent cases (see e.g. *Baxter* v. *Four Oaks Properties Ltd* (1965)) but the essential feature remains: **there must have been a common intention that the purchaser would be subject to mutual restrictions which are reciprocal**, i.e. a local law.

SUMMARY OF SITUATION FIVE

The effect of combining the rule that a party can be bound in equity by a negative covenant (Aidan) with the rule that in equity a party can claim the benefit of a covenant (Eileen) is that Eileen can sue Aidan for breach of the covenant not to run a business on Blackacre.

Now that we have looked at the enforceability of covenants between both the parties and subsequent parties there are two more issues to consider. Neither requires a detailed knowledge for most examinations but both need a mention.

■ Discharge of covenants

KEY STATUTORY PROVISION

Section 84(1)(a) of the LPA 1925

The Lands Tribunal has power 'wholly or partly to discharge or modify' a restrictive covenant.

There are several grounds for this: e.g. that the covenant is obsolete; that it impedes reasonable use of the land; that the removal of the covenant would not injure those entitled to any benefit; or that they have agreed to the removal of the covenant.

■ Remedies for breach of a restrictive covenant

EXAM TIP

Do not forget to mention remedies at the end of your answer. Students often do so and lose marks as a result.

❚ Injunction.
❚ Damages in lieu of an injunction.

An **injunction** is a court order which either orders a lawful act to be done or restrains an unlawful act.

❚Possible reform of the law

Look at the proposals in the Law Commission Report: *Transfer of Land: The Law of Positive and Restrictive Covenants* No 127, 184. A reference to possible defects on the law and proposals for change can make your answer stand out from the rest!

Chapter summary
Putting it all together

Answer guidelines

See problem question at the start of the chapter.

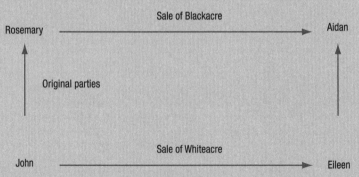

1 Action by Eileen against Aidan. Eileen must prove that:
  ▌ Her land has the benefit of the covenants.
  ▌ Aidan's land has the burden of the covenants.
2 Consider Aidan (b) first:
  ▌ **Covenant (a):** Negative (*Tulk* v. *Moxhay* (1848)) so burden may pass – go through conditions for this to happen (*LCC* v. *Allen* (1914) etc.) and note also that the covenants must be registered. The question says that title to the land is registered and so answer for only registered land. If the question does not say whether it is registered, then answer for both registered and unregistered land.

- **Covenant (b)**: Positive (*Austerberry* v. *Oldham Corporation* (1885)) so Aidan cannot be bound, although Rosemary remains liable on the covenant.
- **Covenant (c)**: *Halsall* v. *Brizell* (1957) situation.

3 Now consider Eileen:
- Eileen can sue Aidan under (a) if the benefit has passed to her in equity. The covenants are expressed to be made for the benefit of Whiteacre, so this may be enough (see *Rogers* v. *Hosegood* (1900)) but in any case on the basis of *Federated Homes* v. *Mill Lodge Properties* (1980) (applying s.78(1) of the LPA 1925) there is probably statutory annexation.
- Eileen can sue Aidan under (c) under the benefit–burden principle.

4 Finally, **do not forget remedies**: injunction plus damages?

Making your answer stand out
Look at each of these points:

- Uncertainty if *Halsall* v. *Brizell* applies.
- Application of s.56(1) LPA thrown in, e.g. 'The covenants are expressed to be for the benefit of Blackacre and adjacent land'.
- Personal covenant as well, e.g. covenant not to allow children to live on the land.

11
Mortgages

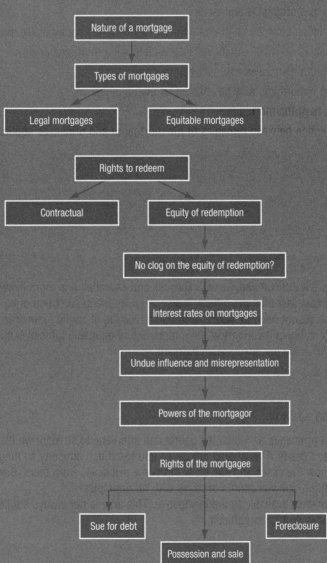

Revision checklist

What you need to know:

- [ ] Mortgages as proprietary interests in land
- [ ] Mortgages as contracts
- [ ] When a mortgage is legal
- [ ] When a mortgage is equitable
- [ ] Distinction between contractual right to redeem and equity of redemption
- [ ] Principles on which equity will intervene to set a mortgage aside
- [ ] When interests rates may be held unconscionable
- [ ] When a mortgage may be affected by undue influence
- [ ] Powers of the mortgagor
- [ ] Distinction between remedies of the mortgagor and principles applicable to each

Introduction
Understanding mortgages

This topic is not difficult and, as with licences and estoppel, it is more heavily weighted to case law than the others. It also involves the intervention of equity and, although you do not need to have a detailed knowledge of equity to answer these questions, it will help if you stress the importance of equitable principles such as the need to strike down unconscionable bargains.

Essay question advice

Essays may deal with:

- General principles on which the courts can intervene to strike down clauses in mortgage deeds. This should not cause you too much difficulty so long as you both know the cases and can draw out some principles from them. Beware of just putting down accounts of cases with no principles!
- The remedies available to the mortgagee. This area is not always studied by candidates, but is not difficult.

Problem question advice

Problem questions usually involve a number of clauses in a mortgage which you need to examine to see if they are liable to be struck down on the grounds that they are oppressive, unconscionable, etc. A sound knowledge of the cases is needed but this is an area on which you should aim to score highly.

The problem may also involve undue influence although this can arise in an equity exam.

Sample questions

Could you answer these questions? Have a look at the questions which follow. They are examples of a typical essay question and a typical problem question. This chapter will cover the issues raised in these questions and review the law necessary to provide a comprehensive answer. Guidelines on answering the problem question will be provided at the end of the chapter and guidelines on answering the essay question are on the companion website for this book.

Essay question

'To what extent is a mortgagor who defaults protected by English law?'

Problem question

John holds a 21-year legal lease of a petrol station. The lease began on 1 January 2004. On 1 January 2006 John mortgaged the lease to Gas Ltd, an oil company, in return for a loan of £100,000.

The mortgage deed provides that:

(a) The loan will be repaid by stated instalments over a period of 18 years and John is not permitted to repay earlier.

(b) At the end of 18 years Gas Ltd can purchase the remainder of the lease at a price to be agreed between the parties and, in default of agreement, it will be settled by an independent valuer.

(c) If John is late by one day or more in paying any instalment then he will have to pay an extra 5% interest on all subsequent instalment repayments.

(d) The rate of interest for the whole period of the loan will be 15%.

John's business has done better than expected and he wishes to pay off the loan now free from these conditions. Advise him on his legal position.

■ Nature of a mortgage

Note: terminology: do remember that the lender is the **mortgagee** and the borrower is the **mortgagor**.

The simple idea of a mortgage is that it is security for a loan. In fact, a mortgage is both:

■ a contract between the mortgagor and the mortgagee; *and*
■ a proprietary interest in the land of the mortgagor granted to the mortgagee.

If a mortgage was only a contract then this would not give the mortgagee enough security, because if the land was sold then the new owner would not be bound to repay the mortgage. Therefore, it must also give an interest in the land.

■ Types of mortgage

A mortgage of land is normally a charge by deed by way of legal mortgage. This will be legal but an equitable mortgage can be created by an agreement which complies with s.2 of the Law of Property (Miscellaneous Provisions) Act 1989.

REVISION NOTE

Check in Chapter 1 that you can recall these provisions.

■ Rights to redeem

Redemption of the mortgage means simply paying it off so that the land is free from the mortgage. There are two rules here:

Date of mortgage | Contractual date: usually six months later | Equity of redemption now takes over

FURTHER THINKING

Equity played a major part in developing the law on mortgages and this is for historical reasons. Mortgages were traditionally entered into when someone needed a loan because they were in debt and so they might be persuaded into a mortgage on terms which were very onerous. This is why equity aimed to protect them. One way was to allow redemption beyond the contractual date and this is known as the equity of redemption. Today mortgages are usually made not because the borrower is in desperate need of money but because a person wishes to buy or lease a house. However, equity still insists on the equity of redemption and it also claims the right to set a mortgage aside (see below) which would not be the case if only the common law applied. The idea of equitable intervention is dealt with below. Read Oldham in Tee (ed.) *Land Law: Issues, Debates, Policy* (Willan Publishing, 2002) pp. 167–210.

Problem area

The extent to which the courts can intervene to set aside the terms of a mortgage. This is a fundamental issue in exam questions because:

(a) It can arise in an essay.

(b) You can gain extra marks in answering problem questions by not just quoting cases which deal with the particular point, but stressing that, in the background, there is a debate on the precise extent to which the courts can intervene.

A good starting point is the words of Greene MR in *Knightsbridge Estates Trust Ltd* v. *Byrne* (1939) (below) 'But equity does not reform commercial transactions because they are unreasonable. It is concerned to see two things – one that the essential requirements of a mortgage transaction are observed, and the other that oppressive or unconscionable terms are not enforced.'

Note the distinction drawn by Greene MR between 'unreasonable' and 'oppressive or unconscionable'. This is easy to remember and apply in an exam question.

However, you must also point out that the cases do not always follow this principle. This is because there are relics of old doctrines which were based on the idea that the only reason why mortgages were entered into was because the mortgagor was desperate for money and so could easily be taken advantage of. However, mortgages are taken out today, to buy houses, from large building societies and other financial institutions which are subject to statutory regulation. When you read the cases below, bear this point in mind.

FURTHER THINKING

Read the discussion on the above point in N. Gravells *Land Law: Text and Materials* (Sweet & Maxwell, 3rd edn, 2004) pp. 912–13 and the discussion on 'clogging the equity of redemption' below.

■ Equity of redemption

A fundamental principle is that the mortgagor must be able to redeem early. However, as this is equity this is not an absolute rule.

KEY CASE

Knightsbridge Estates v. *Byrne* [1939] Ch 441

Concerning: early redemption of a mortgage

Facts

A commercial mortgage at ordinary interest rates where there was no inequality of bargaining power provided that it could not be redeemed for 40 years. The borrower wished to repay earlier, as interest rates had fallen. They were not allowed to redeem early.

Legal principle

There is no absolute rule that a mortgagee can always be allowed to redeem the mortgage early.

However, early redemption would be allowed in domestic mortgages and different considerations apply to leases.

KEY CASE

Fairclough v. *Swan Brewery* Co. Ltd [1912] AC 565

Concerning: when the postponement of the right to redeem a mortgage is void

Facts

The mortgagor was an assignee of a lease which had 17½ years to run. The final mortgage instalment was due only six weeks before the lease expired.

Legal principle

Where the redemption date of the mortgage on a lease is at the point when the lease is about to expire, then redemption is of no value to the mortgagor. Therefore, the mortgagor was entitled to redeem earlier.

■ No clog on the equity of redemption

This principle is easily misunderstood. It means that, on redemption, all mortgage obligations must be discharged, but in fact the courts have not always applied this rule rigidly.

Kreglinger v. *New Patagonia Meat and Cold Storage Co. Ltd* [1914] AC 25

Concerning: can a collateral advantage in a mortgage continue after it has been redeemed?

Facts

A firm of woolbrokers lent money on a mortgage which could be repaid at any time in the next five years. The mortgagor also agreed to give the mortgagee first refusal on all their sheepskins and to pay commission on any sold to a third party. This agreement was to last for the full five years. This collateral agreement was upheld.

Legal principle

A collateral advantage for the mortgagee may be upheld where it does not prevent the mortgagor getting his land back in the same form as when it was mortgaged.

Equity also regards a term of the mortgage that gives the mortgagee an option to purchase as a clog on the equity of redemption.

Samuel v. *Jarrah Timber and Wood Paving Corpn Ltd* [1904] AC 323

Concerning: option to purchase in a mortgage

Facts

The mortgage provided that the mortgagee had the right to buy all or any of the mortgaged property.

Legal principle

Such a provision in a mortgage is void.

The House of Lords came to this conclusion with reluctance and it may reconsider this rule in future. Compare *Reeve* v. *Lisle* (1902), where the term was in a separate agreement and was upheld.

Another instance of a clog on the equity of redemption is provided by:

KEY CASE

Noakes & Co. Ltd v. *Rice* [1902] AC 24

Concerning: tie agreement in a mortgage

Facts

The owner of a public house who had mortgaged it to a brewery covenanted to buy all his beer from it and this covenant was to last until after the mortgage was redeemed.

Legal principle

Tie agreements which last after the mortgage has been redeemed are likely to be held invalid.

■ Interest rates on mortgages

These are subject to the general principle that equity will set aside a bargain which is oppressive and unconscionable.

KEY CASE

Cityland and Property (Holdings) Ltd v. *Dabrah* [1968] Ch 166

Concerning: interest rates on a mortgage

Facts

£2,900 was lent but the sum repayable was £4,553 – a premium of 57%. The court took account of the relative strength of the parties, the lack of explanation for the large premium and its size, and held that it was unconscionable.

Legal principle

The courts can strike down interest rates which are unconscionable.

This is not an absolute principle. Compare *Multiservice Bookbinding Ltd* v. *Marden* (1978).

KEY STATUTORY PROVISION

Sections 137–139 of the Consumer Credit Act 1974

The courts have power to re-open a mortgage agreement which is extortionate where the mortgagor is an individual.

EXAM TIP

Check whether the lender is an individual or a company. If the latter, then this Act will not apply.

■ Undue influence and mortgages

Undue influence is a doctrine that, by its nature, is difficult to define precisely but in essence it aims to prevent the vulnerable from exploitation. It is really directed at the manner in which a transaction is entered into.

The essential question to ask is: did the claimant know not only what they were doing but why they were doing it? *Stevens* v. *Leeder* (2005).

You should check whether it is likely to be examined in Land Law, as it can also arise in an Equity exam, but it is certainly relevant to mortgages.

Class 1: Actual (or express) undue influence

This is where undue influence must be proved. Here it is necessary for the claimant to prove that she entered into the transaction not of her own free will but through the exercise of undue influence on her of another.

Class 2: Presumed undue influence

Here the claimant must establish a relationship of trust and confidence between him and the wrongdoer, together with the existence of a transaction that appeared to result in some unfair advantage to the alleged wrongdoer. This then brings the presumption into play so that it is up to the alleged wrongdoer to prove that there was no undue influence.

Having established that there is a relationship of trust and confidence, Class 2 is then subdivided into:

- **Class 2A**. These are traditional situations where equity has presumed a relationship of trust and confidence and so where a transaction is entered into by the 'weaker' party in favour of the 'stronger' one, then undue influence is presumed.

  The main situations are: parent and child; doctor and patient; clergy and parishioner; trustee and beneficiary.

- **Class 2B**. These are other situations where the claimant establishes that she reposed trust and confidence in the alleged wrongdoer. Once this is done and the transaction is shown to have resulted in some unfair advantage to the claimant, then the presumption applies and the burden shifts.

Note: Class 2B is the most likely area for an exam question on mortgages, as the presumption can arise from any relationship where there is trust and confidence by one party in another.

Lord Nicholls in *Royal Bank of Scotland* v. *Etridge (No. 2)* (2002) provided the following useful test for whether undue influence should be presumed: whether the transaction is *not* readily explicable from the relationship of the parties.

Problem area

Students, for some reason, fail to deal with the presumption point properly. Make sure that, having first decided that this is a possible undue influence case, you then move on immediately to see where in the above categories it falls. This will decide the rest of the case, as it is obviously vital to know whether undue influence has to be proved or not.

Undue influence can affect a mortgage in two ways:

- Where the mortgagee has exercised undue influence to induce the mortgagor to enter into the mortgage. A possible example is:

National Westminster Bank v. *Morgan* **[1985] 1 All ER 821**

Concerning: claim that a mortgage was entered into as a result of undue influence

Facts

A wife claimed that she was induced by the bank (the mortgagee) to sign a mortgage of the matrimonial home, which was in the joint names of herself and her husband, by undue influence on the part of the bank. The object was to secure a loan to the husband. The bank manager visited her house to explain the mortgage to her but it was held that this did not by itself give rise to any special duty on the part of the mortgagee. Nor had the bank manager acquired a dominating influence over her.

Legal principle

The facts did not raise a presumption of undue influence by the bank. In any event, the object of the mortgage, which was jointly signed by the husband, was to save the husband's business which would indirectly benefit the wife.

▮ Where the mortgagee has not exercised undue influence but it is claimed that a third party has and this affects the mortgagee.

Example

X's business is in financial difficulty and he asks his bank for a loan. The bank will only do this if the loan is secured by a charge over the house which is in the joint names of X and his wife Y. The bank gives the documents creating the charge to X and tells him to get Y to sign them. X exercises undue influence over Y to get her to sign. The bank may be affected by this.

▮Undue influence and third parties

This area has become of great importance in recent years, especially since the decision of the House of Lords in *Barclays Bank plc* v. *O'Brien* (1995). This case has really led to a new area of equitable intervention and can be seen as one example of the modern renaissance of equity.

Example

John persuades Claude, his partner, to enter into a second mortgage of their jointly owned home to the Viper Bank in order to secure some business debts of John. It is clear that John exercised undue influence over Claude to persuade him to sign. The question is whether the Viper Bank is affected by what John has done. If it is not, then, although John may be liable to Claude, the actual mortgage is unaffected.

Barclays Bank plc v. *O'Brien* [1995] 1 All ER 438

Concerning: when can a lender be put on notice of the undue influence or misrepresentation of another

Facts

A wife executed a charge securing her husband's unlimited guarantee of a company's liability to a bank. He had misrepresented to her that it was just a temporary security for £60,000.

Legal principle

She was not liable.

A lender will be put on notice if the transaction is not to the financial advantage of the wife *and* there is a substantial risk that the husband has committed a legal or equitable wrong in persuading the wife to enter into the transaction. *If so*, the lender has constructive notice of any rights which the wife may have to set aside the transaction.

FURTHER THINKING

The judgment of Lord Browne-Wilkinson in this case is relatively short and clear. Do read it, especially as it will lead you on to the issues in the next case.

This principle also extends to cohabitants and other relationships, where one party in the relationship (the 'weaker' party) enters into a transaction that is not to their financial advantage. Even so, judgments still refer to just 'wives' as does the judgment in the next case.

KEY CASE

Royal Bank of Scotland v. _Etridge (No. 2)_ [2002] UKHL 44, [2002] 2 AC 773

Concerning: steps which a lender should take to avoid being affected by the undue influence of another, e.g. the borrower

Legal principle

The furthest the lender can be expected to go is to take reasonable steps to satisfy itself that the wife appreciated the practical implications of the proposed transaction. The lender must explain that it will require confirmation from the solicitor who has advised the wife and the lender must see a certificate from the person who gave the independent advice (e.g. a solicitor) confirming that advice has been given, but it does not have to satisfy itself that the advice was correct.

FURTHER THINKING

The principle in _O'Brien_ and the decision in _Etridge_ (above) have been the subject of a great deal of academic debate. A good place to start is the article by Andrews 'Undue Influence–Where's the disadvantage?' (2002) Conv 456.

Consequences of undue influence

If the mortgage is affected by undue influence then it is voidable, i.e. it can be set aside.

Problem area

There has been debate about the extent to which the mortgage is set aside: in _TSB Bank plc_ v. _Camfield_ (1995) the whole mortgage was set aside, but in _Dunbar Bank plc_ v. _Nadeem_ (1997) it was set aside only on condition that the claimant accounted to the mortgagee for the benefit which she had had from it.

▮ Misrepresentation and mortgages

Instead of, or in addition to, the possibility of undue influence, an exam question may ask you if there has been misrepresentation. You will not need to remember much on this from your contract days, just the definition:

KEY DEFINITION

A **misrepresentation** is an untrue statement of fact which induces a person to enter into a transaction.

Look out for where undue influence and misrepresentation are possibly combined: i.e. X uses undue influence to persuade Y, his partner, to sign a mortgage but also lies about how much the mortgage is for.

Rights of the mortgagee

Sue for debt

This is a contractual right and allows the mortgagee to recover the debt.

Possession and sale

This allows the mortgagor to take possession (the mortgage deed allows this at any time during the mortgage) and to sell the property. Any surplus belongs to the mortgagee.

FURTHER THINKING

Section 36 of the Administration of Justice Act 1970 allows the court a discretion to postpone sale. Look at *Cheltenham and Gloucester Building Society* v. *Norgan* (1996) for the principles on which this should be exercised.

Foreclosure

This is rarely granted – it vests the property in the mortgagee and the mortgagor has no right to any surplus.

Chapter summary
Putting it all together

Answer guidelines

See the problem question at the start of the chapter.

John
(mortgagor) ──────────────────────────────► Gas Ltd
(mortgagee)

Terms of mortgage. Binding or not?

(a) Oppressive? *Knightsbridge* v. *Byrne* (1939) should be mentioned and discuss why unlikely to apply. Likely to be held void.

(b) Void. *Samuel* v. *Jarrah* (1904).

(c) Oppressive?

(d) Similarly likely to be held oppressive. Consumer Credit Act ss.137–139 may apply – is the rate extortionate?

Conclusion

Make sure that, before you go into the exam, you:

- [ ] Go through each case in the text and make sure that you know the legal principle of each. You may find it helpful to make a separate list of these cases, write down the name of each and under it leave space for you to write in the legal principle. Facts of cases are only relevant when they explain the principle – never in themselves.

- [ ] Remember that:
  - Land Law exams do not require you to recall vast numbers of cases.
  - Land Law exams do require you to be accurate and precise. This means that you must be absolutely clear about the point of a case.

- [ ] Do the same for statutes. Concentrate on the legal principle and remember to use the facts to illustrate the principle. Extract the key words of a statute and learn them.

- [ ] Do the same for all the key definitions.

- [ ] Remember the Land Law box at the beginning of this book? Go back to it and make sure that you understand how each part fits together and remember that, when revising, you cannot leave out the fundamentals of this subject. Here is an example:

Example

You decide that registered land is not for you and so you leave it out when revising. However, you decide to concentrate on easements, adverse possession and leases. When you come to each topic you immediately run up against land registration principles: is the lease an overriding interest; does an equitable easement have to be registered; how does an adverse possessor become registered? You cannot answer these questions without a knowledge of the principles of registered land. Remember too that questions have a nasty habit of asking you whether it would make any difference to your answer if title was unregistered and so you also need to know this. You also cannot, of course, escape knowing the difference between legal and equitable interests in Chapter 1.

Some final advice:

In any question, make absolutely sure that:

▌ You know what the right is.
▌ You know if it is a proprietary right or a personal one.
▌ You know how it should be created and can identify how it was actually created in the situation in the question.
▌ You know how it fits into the scheme of registered and unregistered land.

If you make sure that you can answer these questions for each topic then you have an excellent framework for an answer. Do not crowd out your answer with too much detail: make the fundamental principles, clearly explained and applied, stand out. Remember that Land Law is a jigsaw. All the pieces do fit and, when you have worked out how they do, you will be fascinated by Land Law for ever! Good luck!

Glossary of terms

Key definitions

Absolute	Appears to have no meaning beyond the fact that a term of years may be absolute even if it contains a clause enabling either party to determine it by notice.
Bare licence	Licence given without any consideration from the licensee i.e. when you are invited to someone's house for a party.
Contractual licence	Where a licence is given for consideration.
Covenants	Promises in a deed.
Easement	Gives a person the right to use the land of another in some way or to prevent it from being used for certain purposes e.g. rights of way and rights of water and light.
Equitable	Means that a right was originally only recognised by the Court of Chancery, which dealt with equitable rights, and not by the Courts of Common Law.
Equitable interests	Not binding on a *bona fide* purchaser for value without notice.
Estate in land	An estate in land refers to the rights which a person has to control and use the land. An estate owner is often called the owner of the land.
Estate owner	Often called the owner of the land.
Estoppel	Arises where one person (the representee) has been led to act on the representation of another (the representor). If so, and if the representee then acts to their detriment on the basis of this promise, then in equity the court may grant them a remedy.
Fee simple absolute in possession	This term means: fee – can be inherited; simple – by anyone; absolute – will not end on a certain event, i.e. to X until he marries; in possession – not e.g. to X at 21.
Injunction	A court order which either orders a lawful act to be done or restrains the doing of an unlawful act.
Interest in land	A right which a person has over another's land.

Joint tenancy	Exists where there are no shares, i.e. all the joint tenants own all the land jointly.
Lease	A lease is an estate in the land which therefore gives a proprietary interest in the land. It must be distinguished from a licence which only gives a personal right in the land.
Legal interest	Legal interests are binding on all the world, i.e. everyone who buys the land.
Licence	Permission from an owner of land (licensor) to the licensee to use the land for a specific purpose.
Licence coupled with a grant	Where the licence is linked to an interest in the land e.g. a licence to go on to land to collect wood. The right to collect wood is a profit.
Misrepresentation	An untrue statement of fact which induces a person to enter into a transaction.
Mortgage	A charge on land to secure a debt.
Negative covenant	A covenant which restricts the use to which land can be put.
Overreaching	The process by which equitable rights which exist under a trust of land are removed from the land and transferred to the money (called capital money) which has just been paid to purchase the land. The effect is to give the purchaser automatic priority over equitable interests under a trust.
Overriding interest	An unregistered disposition which overrides registered dispositions.
Positive covenant	A covenant which requires the covenantor to spend money.
Prescription	Acquisition of easements and profits by long use.
Profit	Gives the right to take something from the land of another e.g. peat, fish, wood or grazing rights.
Protected registered interests	Any interests which are not overriding and include: restrictive covenants, legal and equitable easements and profits, estate contracts and rights of beneficiaries under a trust.
Registrable disposition	A disposition that must be completed by registration.
Restrictive covenant	A restrictive covenant exists where a person covenants in a deed not to use his land in a certain way or to do something on his land e.g. to keep fences in repair or not to build on the land.
Severance in equity	Such acts or things as would, in the case of personal estate, ever the tenancy in equity.
Specific performance	A court order which commands the performance of a contract.
Tenancy in common	Exists where the owners have shares in the land.
Term of years	Any period having a fixed and certain duration.
Trust	A trust arises when property is held by one person (the trustee) on trust for another (the beneficiary).

Other terms

Assignment	Transfer of property such as, in Land Law, a lease.
Beneficiaries	Those who are entitled in equity to property which is held on trust and who therefore have the equitable (beneficial) interest in that property.
Commonhold	A method of holding freehold land used to enable the owners of flats to form a company which will hold the common parts (e.g. the stairs) as commonhold.
Covenant	An obligation contained in a deed.
Deed	An instrument which makes it clear on its face that it is intended to be a deed and which satisfies the requirements for execution as a deed.
Equity	The body of rules developed and administered by the Court of Chancery.
Freehold	A legal estate held in fee simple absolute in possession.
Leasehold	A legal estate held as a term of years absolute.
Mortgagee	Lender in a mortgage.
Mortgagor	Borrower in a mortgage.
Obiter	An observation made in a judgment which is not part of the actual decision in the case and so is not a precedent (in full, obiter dicta) but is often used as a guide to what the law might be.
Paper owner	The holder of the legal title to land which is being adversely possessed.
Periodic tenancy	A tenancy for a certain period (weekly, monthly, quarterly etc) which is automatically renewed at the end of each period unless either party gives notice.
Registered proprietor	The person who is registered as the proprietor of land to which the title has been registered.
Rentcharge	A sum, payable at periodic intervals, which is charged on freehold land.
Severance	Where something is divided up e.g. where a joint tenancy is divided into separate shares so that it becomes a tenancy in common.
Trustees	Those who hold property on trust for others who are the beneficiaries.

Index